Essence of Bharatanatyam

English Language
Essence of Bharatanatyam
(Reference)
by
Kalamandalam Sheeba Krishnakumar

Published in October 2023
by Decan Imprint Publishing Co.
Reg. Off: Sharjah Publishing City
Free Zone Sharjah, UAE.
Phone: 00971-551830334
Email : decanimprint@gmail.com

Cover Design : Prasanth Mangad

Printed at
Printing Park, Tly

12/23-24/Sl.No.12/250/NS 15.4
ISBN 978-93-5973-433-0

Essence of Bharatanatyam

Kalamandalam Sheeba Krishnakumar

DECANIMPRINT

PREFACE

"Essence of Bharathanatyam" invites you to embark on a captivating exploration of this exquisite art form. From its origins in the temples of ancient India to its modern- day renaissance on global stages, Bharathanatyam has evolved, yet its core essence remains unchanged-a profound celebration of life, devotion, and storytelling.

In this book, we delve deep into the intricate mudras, graceful adavus, and intricate abhinaya that define Bharathanatyam. We uncover the spiritual and cultural significance embedded in every movement, every expression, and every note of the accompanying music. As you turn the pages, you'll discover the dedication, discipline, and passion that dancers invest in mastering this art, transforming it into a form of transcendence.

"The Essence of Bharathanatyam" is not just a book but a tribute to the soul-stirring magic that unfolds when a dancer surrenders to the divine rhythm of the dance. Whether you are a novice eager to understand the basics or a seasoned performer seeking to deepen your appreciation, this book promises to be your guide on this enchanting journey.

Prepare to be enchanted, enlightened, and enraptured as we unlock the profound and timeless essence of Bharathanatyam-a dance that transcends time, borders, and cultures.

INTRODUCTION

Welcome to the captivating world of Bharatanatyam! This book is a journey into the heart and soul of one of India's most revered classical dance forms, a tradition that has enthralled audiences for centuries. In the following pages, we will delve into the essence of Bharatanatyam, exploring its rich history, intricate techniques, and profound cultural significance.

Bharatanatyam: A Celebration of Movement and Emotion seeks to provide both newcomers and aficionados with a comprehensive understanding of this ancient art. Whether you are an aspiring dancer, a curious reader, or someone eager to appreciate the beauty of Indian culture, this book will guide you through the enchanting world of Bharathanatyam.

Significance of Bharatanatyam: Bharatanatyam is not just a dance; it is a profound expression of India's cultural heritage and spiritual essence. Rooted in the sacred temples of South India, this classical dance form embodies a sacred connection between art and devotion. Its origins trace back to the ancient text Natya Shastra, where dance was considered a divine offering to the gods. As a classical Indian dance form, Bharatanatyam epitomizes the synthesis of various art forms: music, poetry, drama, and sculpture. Through intricate footwork, graceful movements, and expressive storytelling, Bharatanatyam artists communicate complex narratives and emotions, transcending language barriers to convey universal human experiences.

This dance form is characterized by its precise hand gestures, known as mudras, and its ability to evoke the Navarasanine essential emotions, from love to anger to compassion. It is a unique mode of storytelling where every gesture, every step, and every expression carries profound meaning.

Bharatanatyam has transcended geographical boundaries, captivating audiences worldwide with its aesthetics and spiritual depth. It has become a symbol of India's cultural richness and has inspired countless individuals to delve into its world, whether as performers, scholars, or passionate enthusiasts. In the pages that follow, we will unravel the layers of Bharatanatyam, from its historical roots to its contemporary relevance, from its technical intricacies to its spiritual significance. So, join us on this extraordinary journey as we explore the essence of Bharatanatyam, a timeless and vibrant gem of classical Indian art.

Self-Introduction

Greetings, dear readers,I am Kalamandalam Sheeba Krishnakumar, a name intricately woven into the rich tapestry of Indian classical dance. From the tender age of eight, I embarked on a remarkable journey through the captivating world of dance, and today, I am honored to share with you the essence of my life long dedication to the art of indian classical dance. My journey commenced at the renowned Kerala Kalamandalam, where I took my first steps in the world of performing arts while still in the 8th standard. This early commitment laid the foundation for an illustrious career that has spanned decades. Along this path, I pursued a Master's degree in English and embarked on a journey towards a Ph.D. in Mohiniyattam, all under the esteemed guidance of Kerala Kalamandalam.

I am not merely a dancer but a performer, a choreographer, a teacher, and an author. I have been fortunate to share my knowledge and passion for classical dance with countless students, many of whom have gone on to shine in their own right. My choreographic creations have sought to blend tradition with innovation, pushing the boundaries of this ancient art form while preserving its soul.

Beyond the stage, I am a devoted wife and a loving mother, and my roots are firmly planted in the culturally vibrant town of Thalassery, Kannur, Kerala. It is here that my family and I have found our home and our inspiration. Throughout my journey, I have been humbled and honored to receive several prestigious awards, including the Kerala Sangeetha Nataka Academy Award in 2022, the Keralakshethra Kala Academy Puraskaram in 2020, and many others. These recognitions have not only celebrated my contributions but have also encouraged me to continue my pursuit of excellence in the world of classical dance.

One of my most cherished achievements is the revival of the forgotten art form known as Ashtapadiyattam, a cultural gem from Kerala's past. With dedication and passion, I, along with my gurus Padmasri Guru Chemenchery Kunhiraman Nair and Kannur Seethalakshmi, brought this art form back to life, ensuring that it retained its original grandeur. This revival culminated in a public performance at Dinesh Auditorium, Kannur, on the 23rd of May, 2017. Since then, this art form has graced stages across India, with over a hundred performances to its credit.

As I pen the pages of Essence of Bharatanatyam, it is my fervent hope that you will join me on this journey through the profound art form that has defined my life. Through this book, I seek to share not only the physical aspects of Bharatanatyam but also its spiritual and cultural significance. I wish to convey the deep emotions and stories that this dance form has the power to express.

This book is not just for aspiring artists and students of Bharatanatyam but for anyone who seeks to appreciate the richness of this art form. It is an ode to Bharatanatyam, a dance that has not only been my life's work but also my life's love.

I extend my heartfelt gratitude to each one of you for joining me on this journey. Your support and interest in the world of Bharatanatyam are truly inspiring. May 'Essence of Bharatanatyam' kindle a deep appreciation for this divine art form in your hearts and continue to illuminate the world of dance for generations to come.

With warm regards,

Kalamandalam Sheeba Krishnakumar

FORWARD

The book in your hand, 'Essence of Bharatanatyam', penned by Kalamandalam Sheeba Krishnakumar of bharatanatya fame and Disciple of late kathakali and dance maestro Padmasree.Guru Chemmancheri Kunhiraman Nair, deals with the intricate nuances and components of the classical art-form bharatanatya based on the Natyasastra of Sage Bharata which emphasizes on the two essential segments known as Lokadharmi and Natyadharmi. The theme of the book consists of mystical, ritualistic and mythological characters and situations in their life. The fundamental components that demand the exposition of nayaka and nayaki laksanas are dwelt in detail in a very powerful and simple style. There are convincing discussions on different types of communication through distinctive hand-gestures, eye contacts and swift movements of the body. The body's flexibility and distinct ability to express different feelings and emotions are focal points in determining the success of the stage production process. The invaluable merits of bharatanatya are its power to communicate the rich Indian cultural heritage and project its universal appeal and outreach. The book explores the immense potential of the play. The role of orchestration in bharatanatya recital is highlighted in the work with 33 segments, each focusing on rhythmic continuity in harmony and liquid music. It is fervently hoped that this unique work will enrich and revive a new interest in the minds of bharatanatya lovers the world over and attract a wide readership.

Prof. Amballoor Appukkuttan
'Sreepadam'

Amballoor   Amballoor

16.10.2023   Ernakulam District, Pin: 682315

INDEX

DHYAN SLOKA

Aangikam bhuvanam yasya,
Vachikam sarva vaangmayam
Aaharyam Chandra thaaraadee
Thun numah saathvikam shivam

Meaning: We bow to the Lord shiva, whose body is the whole universe, whose speech is entire world 's language and whose ornaments are the moon, stars, him we worship the serene Lord Shiva.

Angikam	- Body
Bhuvanam	- Universe
Yasya	- Whose
Vaachikam	- Speech
Sarva	- All
Vaangmayam	- Language(sound)
Ahaaryam	- Ornaments
Chandra	- Moon
Thaara	- Star
Aadi	- Etc
Tham	- That
Numas	- Bow
Saathvikam	- Pure
Shivam	- Lord Shiva

NAATYA-KRAMAHA

Aasyenaalmbayeth geetham
Hasthaynaartham pradarshayeth
Chakshurbhyam darshayeth-bhaavam

Paadhaabhyam thaala-machareth
Yathohasthas thatho –drushithi
Yatho drusthis thatho –manaha
Yatho manas thatho- bhaava
Yatho bhaava thatho rasaha

Meaning: The dancer should be able to sing ,to express the meanings through hands (mudras) and emotions through eyes.The dancer should maintain the beat or thaala by his/her feet. Where the hands go the eyes should follow it , where the eyes go the concentration should be there, when the concentration is there, the expression comes out and when the expression is there, there the rasa arises.

NAAYAKA LAKSHANAM (Qualities of hero)

Neethaveneetho madhuraha
Thyaagi-daksha-priyamvadha
Rakthalooka –suchirvaagmee
Rooda vamsha sthirooyuvaa
Budhiyuthsaaha smrithi-pragnya
Kalaa –mana –samanvithaa
Shrudoo –drudashcha
Thaytjasvee shaastra
Chaksharksha –daarmika

Meaning: The hero should be wellbuilt, charming, liberal and an expert in speaking with affection. He should have eloquent speech, controlled behaviour and he should belong to a good family. This young hero should be endowed with intelligence, energy, wisdom, memorypower, skill of arts, didginity, well versed in sacred scienece, good conduct and also an observer of laws.memorypower, skill of arts, didginity, well versed in sacred scienece, good conduct and also an observer of laws.

NAYAKI LAKSHANAM (Qualities of a heroine)

Thanvee –roopavathi-shyamapeenoon

Natha –payoodharaa

Pragalbha sarasaa kaantha

Kushaaala grahamookshayoo

Vishaalalochana geetha

Vidhya –thaalanuvardhini

Paraadhyabhossha-sampanna

Prasanna-mukhapankaja

Yeva –vidhugunoopayatha

Nayaki samudheeritha.

Meaning: She should be slender bodied, beautiful, young with round breast, self confident, witty(smitham) ,pleasing,knowing when to start and when to stop, having large eyes , able to perform in accompaniment of vocal and instrumental music and to observe the proper time beats(thaala) have splendid (expensive) dress and possesing a happy countenance. A girl having all these qualities is called a dancer.

KINKINI LAKSHNANAM (Qualities of bells)

Suswarascha swaroopascha

Sooryshma nakshathra devatha

Kinkinyaha kaamsyarchitha

Yekakaanguli-kaantharam

Bhadhneeya neela shoothreyna
Grandhabishcha drudampunaha
Shathaath –dwayam shaantham
Waapi paadayor natyakaarini

MEANING: The bells mad eof bronze should have pleasant sound.It should be well shaped and have stars as their dieties.It should rmain one finger apart from one another.The dancing girl should bind hundred or two-hundred of them in each of her feet, with blue thread in tight knots.

RANGADEEVATHA-STHUTHI (Stage prayer)

Bharatha –kula-bhaaghya kalike
Bhaavarasaananda parinathaakaaray
Jagadayka mohanakale
Jaya jaya rangaadi –devathay-devi

MEANING: Oh goddess of rangaa stage, victory to thee, though the art pattern of the actor class the embodiment of the joy occuring from the psychological states (bhaavas) and centiments (rasa), your's in the art, that only can charm the whole world, victory to thee.

HASTHABHEDAS

SINGLE HAND GESTURES (Asumyutha hasta viniyogaha)
Pathaaka Stripathaakoo Ardapathaka Karthareemukaha
Mayooraakyoo Ardachandrascha Araala Shukathundakaha
Mushthischa Shikaraakascha Kaptitha Katakaamukaha (3)
Soochi Chandrakala Padmakoosha Sarpashirasthatha

Mrugasheersha Simamukhaha Kaangoolascha Alapamakaha
Chathuroo Bhramarascheiva Hamsaasyo Hamsapakshakaha
Sandamshoo Mukulascheiva Thaamrachoota Trishuulakaha

Pathaaka	- Flag
Tripathaaka	- Triangular flag
Ardapathaka	- Half Flag
Karthareemukaha	- Scissor's head
Mayura	- Peacock
Ardachandra	- Half moon
Araala	- Mudra
Shukathunda	- Parrot's head
Mushti	- Fist
Shikaraakascha	- Peak
Kaptitha	- Wood apple
Katakaamuka	- Head of bangle
Soochi	- Needle (to point something)
Chandrakala	- Crescent moon
Padmakoosha	- Lotus bud
Sarpashiras	- Snake's head
Mrugasheersha	- Deer's head
Simamukha	- Lion's face
Kaangoola	- Jamun fruit
Alapamaka	- Fully bloomed lotus
Chathura	- To say four/square
Bhramari	- Honey bee
Hamsaasya	- Swan's beak
Hamsapaksha	- Swan's wings
Sandamsha	- To repeat or again and again

Mukula   - Flower bud
Thaamrachoota   - Plume of a cock
Trishuula   - Trinity / Trishulam

ASAMYUTHAHASTHAAH

(1) Pathaaka hasta viniyogaha (The usage of pathaaka)

Naatyarambay Vaarivahay Vanay Vathunisheythanay

Kuchasthalay Neshaayaamcha Nadhyaam Amaramandalay

Thurangay Kandanay Vaayavcha Shayanay Gamanoodhyamay

Prathaapaycha Prasaadaycha Chandrikaayam Ghanaadhapay

Kavaatapaatanay Sapthavibhakthyarthay Thrangakay

Veethi pravesha bhavaypee Samathveycha Angaraahakay

Athmaarthay Shapathaychaapee Thooshneebhavaa nidarshnay

Thaalapathraycha Kaydaycha Dravyaa dis sparshanaythathaa

Aashirvaada kriyaayaamcha Nrupasreshtrasya bhaavanay

Thathra thathraythi vachanay Sindhuvthoo Sukrudikramay

Sambhoodanay Puroogaypee Kadgaroopasya dhaaranay

Maasay Samvathsaray Varshdhinay Sammaarjanaythathaa

Yevamardyeshu yujjyanthay Pathaakahasta Bhaavanaahaa.

Naatyaarambha   - Beginning of dance
Vaarivahay   - Rainy clouds
Vanay   - Forest
Nadhyaam   - River
Amaramandala   - To show the heavens
Thuranga   - Horse
Kandana   - To ignore
Vaayu   - Wind
Shayana   - To sleep

Gamanoodhyama — To make an effort to walk

Prathaapa — To praise

Prasaada — To give blessings

Chandrika — Moonlight

Ghanadhapa — Unbearable

Kavaata-paatanam — Closing and opening of the doors

Sapthavibhakthyartham — Mentioning the seven cases

Tharanga `- Water ripples

Veethipravesha – bhava - The act of entering into the street

Samathva — Equality

Angaranaka — Massaging the body

Athmaartham — To show ones ownself

Shapatham — To make an oath

Thooshneem-bhavaa-nidarshnam - To act silence

Thaalapathra — Palm leaf (to write a letter)

Kayday — Shield of a soldier

Dravyaa- dis — sparshanam - Touching the things

Aashirvaada — To give blessings

Kriyaa — To show how to bless

Nrupa- sreshtrasya-
bhaavana — To show an Emperor

Thathra- thathraychi-
vachanam — To say 'this' or 'that'

Sindhu — Waves in a ocean

Sukrudikram — To be good

Sambhoodanam — Addressing

Purogaypee — To move forward

Kadga — Sword

Roopasya	- Form
Dhaarana	- To wear
Maasa	- Month
Samvathsra	- Years
Varshdhina	- Rainy day
Sammaarjana	- To sweep

(2) Tripathaaka hasta viniyogha

Makutay Vukshabhaavashu Vajray Thathathara-vaasavay
Kaytnakee-kusumay Deepay Vanhijwaalaa-vijrumbhanay
Kapoothay Pathralaykhaayam Bhaanaarthay Parivarthakay
Yujyathay Tripathaakooyam Kathithoo Bharathoothamaihee

Meanings : Makuta - Crown

VuksNabhaava	- To denote a tree (with branches)
Vajra	- Thunder bolt (weapon)
Thathathara-vaasava	- Bearer of that weapon (indira)
Kaythakee Kusuma	- Screwpine flower
Deepam	- Lamp
Vanhijwaalaa-vijrumbhana	- Raising flames
Kapootham	- Pigeon
Pathralaya	- To draw designs on the body
Bhaanaartha	- To shoot an arrow
Parivarthaka	- To do circular movements.

(3) Ardhapathaaka hasta viniyougaha

Pallavay Palakay Theeray Ubhayoorithivaachakay
Krakachay Churikaayaamcha Dwajay Goopura- sringayoho
Yujyathay Ardhapathaakooyam Thathakarmaprayoogakay

Meanings :

Pallava	- Tender leaves
Palaka	- Wooden plank
Theera	- River bank
Ubhayoorithivaachaka	- To denote or to say two
Krakacha	- Saw
Churikaa	- Pen-knife
Dwaja	- Flag
Gopura	- Temple tower or any tower
Sringayoho	- Horns

(4) Karthareemukha hasta viniyogaha

Sthreepum- Sayoosthu-vishiashey Viparyaasapadeypivaa

Luntanay Nayanaamtheycha Maranay Bhedabhaavanay

Vidhyudarthey Yekashaiya-virahay Pathnaythatha

Lathaayaam Yujathay Yasthu Sakara Karthareemukhaha

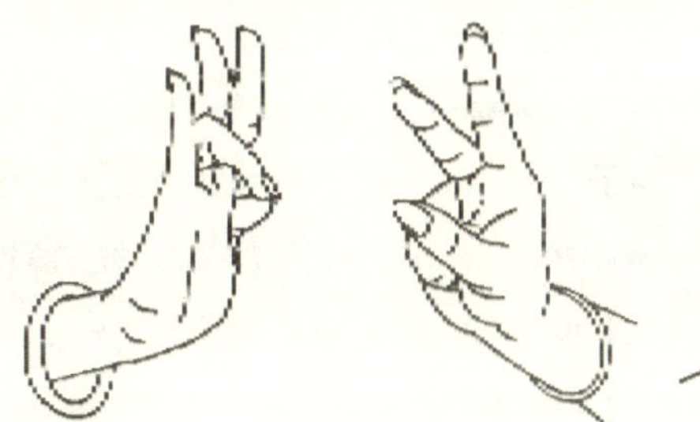

Meanings:

Sthreepum	- The difference between
Sayoosthu-vishiasha	- woman and man
Viparyaasapadeypivaa	- Showing 'this' or 'that'
Luntana	- Rolling
Nayanaamtham	- Corner of the eyes
Marana	- To show death

Bhedabhaavana	- To show the difference of opinions
Vidhyudartha	- Lightning
Yekashaiya - viraha	- To lay one in the bed while in separation from the loved one
Pathana	- To fall down
Lathaa	- Creeper

(5) Mayura hasta viniyogaha

Mayuraasyeh Lathaayaamcha Shakunay Vamanaythathaa

Alkasyaapanayanay Lalaata-thilakay-sucha

Nandhyudakasya-Niksheypay Shaastravaaday Prasindhakay

Yevamardhyeshu Yujyanthay Mayurakara-Bhaavanaahaa

Meanings:

Mayurasyam	- Peacock
Lathaa	- Creepers
Shakunam	- A bird
Vamanam	- To denote vomitting
Alkasyaapanayanam	- To remove the hair knots
Lalaatathilakam	- To put sacred mark on the forehead
Nandhyddakasya-Niksheypam	- Sprinkling water over the head
Shaastravaada	- Discussing about shastras
Prasidhaka	- Very famous

(6) Ardachandra hasta viniyogaha

Chandray Krishnaashtamee bhaajae Galahastaartha kaypicha

Balaayudhay Devathaanaam Abishechanakarmani

Bukpaathray cha Udhbhavay Katyaam Chinthaayam Athmavaachakay

Dhyaanaycha Praarthnaychaapee Angaanamsparshnaythathaa

Praakruthaanam-namaskaaray Ardachandrooiyujyathay

Meanings:

Chandray — The moon on the eighth day after the full moon

Krishnaashtamee - bhaajae

Galahastaartha - Holding somebodies neck and pushing him

Balaayudha - A weapon

Devathaanaam - Abishechana-karmani- Offerings to God

Bukpaathra - Eating plate

Udhbhava - Origin or birth

Katyaam - Waist

Chinthaayaam - Worrying

Athmavaachakam - Musing about one's ownself

Dhyaana - Meditation

Praarthana - Prayers

Angaanaam-sparsha- Touching the limbs

Praarkruthaanaam Namaskaram - To greet common people

(7) Araala hasta viniyogaha

Vishaadyam-amrutha-paanayshu Prachanda-pavanaypicha

Meanings :

Vishaadhyam - To show drinking of poison

amrose - or Amrutham Paanay

Prachanda-pavana - Violent breeze

(8) Shukathundaka hasta viniyogaha

Bhaanaprayogay-kunthaarthay Vaalayasyas-smrithikramay

Marmookthyaam Ugrabhaavaychu

Shukathundooniyujyathay

Meanings:

Bhaanaprayooga	-	Shooting an arrow
Kunthaartha	-	A spear
Alayasyas-smrithikrama	-	Remembering the past
Marmookthyaam	-	Mystic things
Ugrabhaava	-	Great anger

(9) Mushti hasta viniyogaha

Sthiray Kachagarahay Daartyeh Vasthvaadeenaamchadhaaranay

Mallaanaam-yudha-bhaavaypee Mustihasthoya-mishyathay

Meanings:

Sthiram	-	Steadyness
Kachagaraha	-	Grasping one's hair
Daartya	-	Courage
Vasthvaadeenaamcha-dhaarana	-	Holding things
Mallaanaam-yudhabava	-	Fighting mood of wrestlers

(10) Shikara hasta viniyogaha

Madhanay Kaamukay Sthambhay Nischayay Pithrukarmani

Oshtray Pravishtaroopacha Radhanay Prashnabhaavanay

Lingay Naastheethivachanay Smaranay Abhinayaanthikay

Katibhandaakarshnaycha Parirambha-vidikramay

Gantaaninadhay Shikaroo Yujyathay Bharathaadibihi

Meanings:

Madhana	-	Manmaths (God of love)
Kaarmuka	-	Bow
Sthambha	-	Pillar
Nischchaya	-	Certainity
Pithrukarmani	-	Offerings to ancestors
Oshtra	-	Lips

Pravishtaroopa	- To pour a liquid
Radhana	- Teeth
Prashnabhaava	- Questioning
Linga	- Shiva lingam or Phallic symbol
Naastheethivachana	- Saying " I don't know"
Smarana	- Recollection
Abhinayaanthikam	- To do "abhinaya"
Katibhandaakarshna	- To tighten the waist band
Parirambhavidikrama	- Embracing
Gantaaninadha	- Sounding a bell

(11) Kapita hasta viniyogaha

Lakshmyamcheiva Saraswathyam Nataanaam Thaala-dhaaranay

Godhohanay Pranjanaycha Leelaakusuma-dhaaranay

Chelaanchalaadi-grahanay Patasyaivaava-gutanay

Dhoopa-deeparchanay-chaapee Kapitha-samprayujyathay

Meanings:

Lakshmyam	- Goddesses Lakshmi
Saraswathy	- Goddesses Saraswathy
Nataanaam	- Holding cymbals (Nattuvangam)
Thaala dhaarana	
Godhohanam	- Milking cows
Anjanam	- Puttying collyrium
Leelaakusuma-	- Holding flower at the time of lover dhaarana
Chelaanchalaadi	- Grasping the end of a saree grahana
Patasyaivaava-gutana	- Wrapping one's head with a cloth
Dhoopa-deeparchanam	- Offering incense or light

(12) Katakaamuka hasta viniyogaha

Kusumaavachayeh Mukthaa -sraghaamnaam Dhaaranay-thatha

Sharamadhya-karshanaycha Naagavallipradhaanakay
Kasthoori-Kaadivasthoonaam Payshanay Gandhavasanay
Vachanay Drushti-bhaavaypee Katakaamukaha ishyathay

Meanings:

Kusumavacha   - Plucking flowers
Mukthaa-sragha   - A pearl necklace
Dhaaranam   - To wear
Sharamadhya-Karshanam - Drawing the middle of a bow
Naagavallipradhaanam - Offering betal leaves
Kasthoori-Kaadivasthoonaam - Preparing the paste of musk
Payshana   - To mix
Gandhavasana   - To smell
Vachana   - To speak
Drushti   - Glancing

(13) Soochi hasta viniyogaha

Yehkaarthaypee- Parabrahma- Bhaavanaayam Shathaypicha
Ravav Nagaryaam Lookarthay Thatheythi Vachanaypicha
Yachabday-api-thachabdhay Vijanaarthapi Tharjanay
Kaarshyeh Shalaakay Vapushi Aashcharyeh Venibhaavanay
Chathray Samarthay Paanavcha Roomaallyaam Bherivaadhanay
Kulaalachakra-bramanay Rathaanga-mandalaythathaa
Viveychanay Dinaanthaycha Soochi-hasta Prakeerthithaha

Meanings:

Yehkaartha   - Denoting a number
Parabrahma-Bhaavana - Supreme soul 'Brahma'
Shatha   - Denoting a hundred
Ravi   - Sun
Nagarya   - City

Lookartham — World
Thatheythi Vachanam — To say 'like that'
Yachabday-api-thachabdham — Asking "this or that"?
Vijanaartha — Lonely place
Tharjana — To threaten somebody
Kaarshya — Growing thin
Shalaaka — Throne
Vapushi — Body
Aashcharya — Astonishment
Venibhaavana — To show a braid of hair
Chathra — Umbrella
Samartha — Capability
Paanav — Hands
Roomaalyaam — Eye brows
Bherivaadhana — Beating the drums
Kulaalachakra-bramana — Potter's wheel
Rathaanga-mandala — Circumference of a wheel
Viveychana — To Think
Dinaantha — End of the day

(14) Chandrakala hasta viniyogaha

Chandray Mukaycha Praadehshey Thanmaathraa-kaarvasthuni

Shivasya-makutaky Gangaanadhyaamcha Lagudaaypicha

Yehshaam Chandrakalaa-cheiva Viniyoodhyaa Videeyathay

Meanings:

Chandra — Moon
Muka — Face
Praadesha — To show the span between the
thumb & the index finger

Thanmaathraa-kaarvasthuni - To denote objects of that shape

Shivasya-makuta   - Lord Shiva's crown

Gangaanadhyaam   - River Ganga

Lagudaa   - Axe (cut)

(15) Padmakosham hasta viniyogaha

Phalay Bilvakapiththaadhav Sthreenaamcha Kucha-Kummbayoohoo

Aavarthakay Kandhukay Sthaalyaam Bhojanay Pushpakoorakay

Sahakaaraphalay Pushpa-varshey Manjarikaadishu

Japakusumabhavecha Gantaaroopey Vidhaanake

Valmeekay Kamalay Pyanday Padmakoosha Videeyathay

Meanings:

Phalay Bilvakapiththadi - Wood apple and Bilva fruit

Sthreenaan cha-Kuthckumbayoho -   Breast of a lady

Aavartha	-	Circular Movements
Kundhuka	-	Ball (act of playing)
Sthalyam	-	Pot
Bhojana	-	To eat
Pushpakoraka	-	Flower garland
Sahakaaraphala	-	Mango fruit
Pushpa-varsha	-	Showering of flowers
Manjarikaadishu	-	Bunch of flowers
Japakusuma	-	Hibiscus flowers
Gantaaroopa	-	Bell
Vidhanak	-	Image of god
Valmeeka	-	An ant hill
Kamala	-	Lotus
Anda	-	Egg

(16) Sarpashiras Viniyogaha

Chandanay Bhujagay Manthray Prookshanay Pooshanaadishu

Devasyoo-dakadaanayshu Aaspahalay Gajakumbhayoohoo

Bhujasthaanaythu-Mallanaam Yujyathay Sarpasheershakaha

Meanings:

Chandana	- Sandal paste
Bhujaga	- Snake
Manthra	- Low pitch
Prokshana	- Sprnikling
Poshana	- Nourishing
Devasyoo-dakadaane	- Offerings of god
Aaspahala	- Patting
Gajakumbhayoohoo	- Protuverances of an Elephant's head
Bhujasthaanaythu-Mallanaam	- The heavy arms of the wrestlers

(17) Mrugasheersha hasta viniyogaha

Sthreenaamarthey Kapoolaycha Chakra-maryaadhayoorapee

Bheethyaam Vivaaday Naypathyeh Aahvaanaycha Thrupundrakay

Mrugamukay Rangavallyaam Paadasamvahanay Thathaa

Sanchaaraycha Priyahvaanay Yujyathay Mrugasheershakaha.

Meanings:

Sthreenaamarth	- Women
Kapoola	- Cheeks
Chakra	- Wheel
Maryadhayoho	- A limit
Bheethyaam	- Fear
Vivaadam	- Discussing
Naypathya	- Wearing a costume or dressing

Aahvaanay	- Calling
Thrupundraka	- Putting 'Vishnu Nama' on fore-head
Mrugamuka	- Deer's face
Rangavallyaam	- Decorating the floor with rice flour
Paadasamvahana	- Massaging the feet
Sanchaaram	- Walling (Steepping)
Priyahvaana	- Calling the beloved

(18) Simhamukaha hasta viniyogaha

Homay Shashey Gajey Dharbachalanay Padmadaamini Simhaananey Vaidhyapaakay Shodhanay Samprayujyathay

Meanings :

Homa	- Yaga
Shasha	- Hare
Gaja	- An Elephant
Dharbachalana	- The moving of Darba grass
Padmadaamini	- Lotus garland
Simhaanana	- Lion's face
Vaidhyapaaka	- Preparing medicine
Shodhana	- Testing

(19) Kaangoola hasta viniyogaha

Lakuchasyapalay Balakingkinyaam Gantikaarthakay Chakooray Kramukay Balakuchay Kalhaarakaythathaa Chaathakay Naalikeyreycha Kangooloo Yujyathay Karaha

Meanings:

Lakuchasyapala	- To denote 'Lakucha' fruit
Balakingkinyaam	- Bells worn by children
Gantikaa	- Bells
Chakoora	- Partridge

Kramuka	- Beatle nut tree
Balakucha	- Young girls breast
Kalhaaraka	- A white water lily
Chaathaka	- The bird 'chaathakaa'
Naalikera	- Coconut tree

(20) Alapadma hasta Viniyogaha

Vikachaabjey Kapiththaadiphala Chaavarthakay Kuchey

Virahey Mukuray Poornachandray Sowndarya-bhaavanay

Dhammilley Chandra-shaalaayaam Graamay Chodruthakopayoho

Thataakay Shakatay Chakravaakay Kalakalaravay

Slaaganay Solapadmascha Kathithoo Bharathaagamay.

Meanings:

Vikachaabja	- Afully bloomed lotus
Kapiththaadiphala	- Wood apple
Avarthaka	- Circular movements
Kucha	- Breast
Viraha	- Seperation from the beloved
Mukura	- Mirror
Poornachandra	- Full moon
Sowndarya-bhaavana	- To show beauty
Dhammilla	- Hair-knot
Chandra	- Shaalaay- Moon tower
Graama	- Village
Udruthakopa	- Great anger
Thataaka	- Pond
Shakata	- Cart
Chakravaaka	- Abird
Kalakalarava	- Murmuring sound
Slaagana	- Praising

(21) Chathura hasta viniyogaha

Kasthooryaam Kinchidarthaycha Swarney Thaamrey cha Lohakay,

Aardrey Kaydhey Rasaasvadhey Lochanay Varnabhedhanay

Pramaaney Sarasey Mandhagamanay Shakaleekruthey

Ananey Druththailaadav Yujyathey Chathurahakaraha

Meanings:

Kasthoori	-	Musk
Kinchidartha	-	Little (to denote)
Swarna	-	Gold
Thaamra	-	Copper
Lohaa	-	Iron
Aardra	-	Wet
Kaydha	-	Sorrow
Rasaasvada	-	Taste
Lochana	-	Eyes
Varnabhedhana	-	Difference in caste
Pramaana	-	Vow
Sarasa	-	Sweetness
Mandhagamana	-	Walking slowly
Shakaleekrutha	-	To pierce
Anana	-	Face
Druthailaadhi	-	Ghee, Oil, etc.

(22) Bhramari Hasta Viniyogaha

Bhramarecha Shukay Pakshay Saarasay Kokiladhishoo

Bhramarakyascha Hasthoyam Kathitho Barathagamay

Meanings:

Bhramara	-	Bee
Shuka	-	Parrot

Paksha	- Wings of a bird
Saarasa	- Crane
Kokila	- Cuckoo and similar birds

(23) Hamsasya Hasta Viniyogaha

Maangalyeh Soothrabandhey cha Upadesha-vinischayeh

Romanchay Moukthikadhau cha Deepavarthi-prasaranay

Nikashay Mallikadhau cha Chitreh Thallekaneythatha

Dhamasheycha Jalabhandhay cha Hamsasyo Yujyathay karaha

Meanings:

Maangalayeh Soothrabandha - To tie Mangal Sutra

Upadeesha	- Advice or instruct
Vinishcha	- Certainity
Romancha	- Horripilation
Moukthikaadav	- Pearl neck-lace
Deepavarthiprasaarana	- Wick of a lamp
Nikasha	- Touch stone
Mallikaadi	- Jasmine flower and the like
Chithra	- A painting
Thalleykana	- To paint a picture
Dhamsha	- To bite
Jalabhanda	- A dam

(24) Hamsapaksha Hasta Viniyogaha

Shat-sankyaayaam Sethubanday Nakaray Kaanganaythathaa

Pidhaanay Hamsapakshoyam Kathitho Bharathaagamy

Meanings:

Shat-sankya — Denoting number six

Sethubanda — Construction of a bridge

Nakaray Kaanganam — Putting marks

Pidhaana — To cover (or) hide something

(25) Sandamshoo Hasta Viniyogaha

Udharay Bhalidhaanaycha Vranay Keetay Mahaabhey

Archanay Panchasankyaayaam Sandamshaakyoni-yujyathay

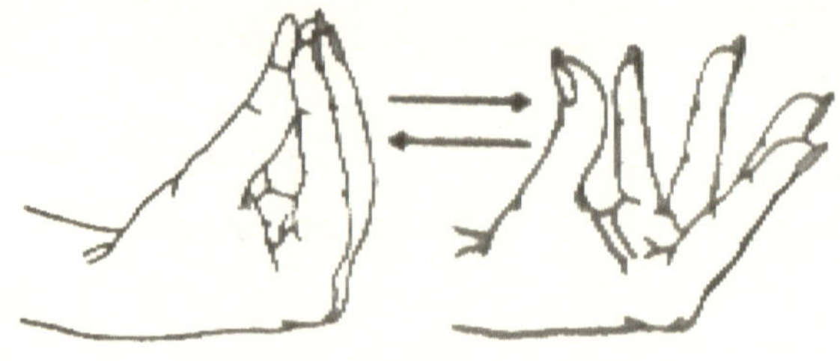

Meanings:

Udhara — Stomach

Bhalidhaana — Offerings to deities

Vrana — A wound

Keeta — Worms

Mahaabahya — Great fear

Archana — Worship

Panchasankya — To denote number five

(26) Mukula Hasta Viniyogaha

Kumudhay Bhoojanay Pancha-bhaanay Mudraadi-dhaaranay

Naabhavcha Kadaleepushpay Yujyathay Mukula-Karaha

Meanings:

Kumudha — Water lily

Bhoojana	- To eat
Pancha-bhaana	- Five flower arrows of 'Manmatha'
Mudhraadi-dhaarana	- Tatoo (seal)
Nabhi	- Navel
Kadhaleepushpa	- Plantain flower

(27) Thaamrachota Hasta Viniyogaha

Kukkutaadhav Bhakay Kaakay Ushtray Vathsay cha Lehkanay

Yujathay Thaamrachoodaakyo Karo-Bharathaadibihee

Meanings:

Kukkuta	- Cock
Bhaka	- Crane
Kaaka	- Crow
Ushtra	- Camel
Vathsa	- Calf
Lehkanam	- Writing instruments

(28) Trishula Hasta Viniyogaha

Bilvapathray Trithvayukthay Trishulakara Yeerithaha

Meanings:

Bilvapathram	- 'Bila' leaves
Trithvayuktham	- Denoting Trinity

DOUBLE HAND GESTURES

Samyutha Hasta Viniyogha

Anjalishcha Kapothascha Karkata Swathikasthathaa

Dolaahasta Pushpaputaha Uthsanga Shivalingakaha

Katakaavardhanascheiva Kartharee-swasthikasthathaa

Shakatam Shanka Chakreycha Samputha Paashaa Keelakav

Matsya Koormoo Varaahascha Garudo Naagabhandhakaha
Katvaa Behrundakaakascha Avathith-thastha-theivacha

Meanings:

Anjali — Namaskar

Kapootha — Pigeon

Karkata — Crab

Swathikam — Swasthik

Dolahasta — Mudra (Related hand posture)

Pushpaputa — Flower holder or basket

Uthsanga — Shoulders

Shivalinga — Shivalingam

Katakaavardhana — Mudra

Kartharee-swasthikastham — Two kartharees in swasthikam

Shakatam — Wheel (Demon's teeth)

Shanka — Conch

Chakram — Chakram (wheel or discuss)

Samputha — Box

Paashaa — A rope (used to show enemity)

Keelakav — Links (used to show affection)

Matsya — Fish

Koorma — Tortoise

Varaaha — Wild pig (or) Boar

Garudo — Eagle (Garudan)

Naagabhandhakaha — Two snakes twisted together

Katvaa — Cot

Berundaka — Berunda bird

Avahith-tha — To hold things in your hand

(1) Anjali hasta viniyogaha

Devathaa-guruvipraanaam Namaskaaray-shvanukramaath

Kaaryaha Shiromukoo-rasthoo Viniyogay Anjalir-Bhudaihee

Meanings:

Namaskaram	- To bow
Devatha	- To God (to bow)
Guru	- To Teacher (to bow)
Vipraanaam	- To Brahmin (to bow)
Kaarya	- Action (doing)
Shiro	- Over the Head near the face
Muka	- Face

(2) Kapotha hasta Viniyogaha

Pranaamay Gurusambhashey Viniyangi-krutheshvayam

Meanings:

Pranaamay	- Offer oblicence
Gurusambhashey	- Discussing with teacher

(3) Karkata hasta Viniyogaha

Samoohaagamaney Thunda-dharshanay Shankapooranay

Angaanaam-mootanay Shaakon-namaneycha-niyujyathay

Meanings:

Samoohaagamana	- A group of Corwd move together
Thunda-dharshana	- To indicate a stomach
Shankapoorana	- To blow the conch
Angaanaam-mootana	- Stretching the limbs of the body
Shaakon-namana	- To pull down the branch

(4) Swasthikam hasta Viniyogha

Samyogeyna Swathi-kaakyo Makaray Viniyujyathay

Meanings:

Samyogeyna   - Joining together

Swathi-kaiya   - With swathikam

Makara   - Show a Crocodile

(5) Dolaa hasta Viniyogaha

Naatyaarambhay Prayookthavya Yethi-Naatya-Vidhoo-Vidhuhu

Meaning:

Naatyaarambhay - Beginning of dance

(6) Pushpaputaha hasta Viniyogaha

Neeraanjanavidav Vaari-phalaadi-grahanaypicha

Sandhyaayaam-ardyadaanaycha Mantra-pushpay cha Yujyathay

Meanings:

Neeraanjanavidav - Showing light before the image of God

Vaari-phalaadi-graha - To take water, fruits, etc.

Sandhyaayaam-ardyadaana - Offering Argya (Water)

Mantra-pushpa - Flower invested with magical power

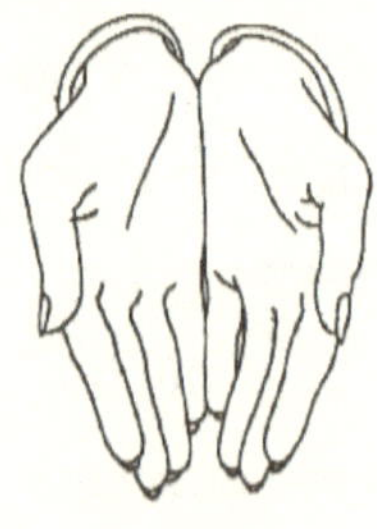

(7) Uthsanga hasta Viniyogaha

Agalinganay cha Lajyaayaam-Angadaadi-Pradarshanay

Baalaanaam-shikshanay Chayamuthsangoo Yujyathay-

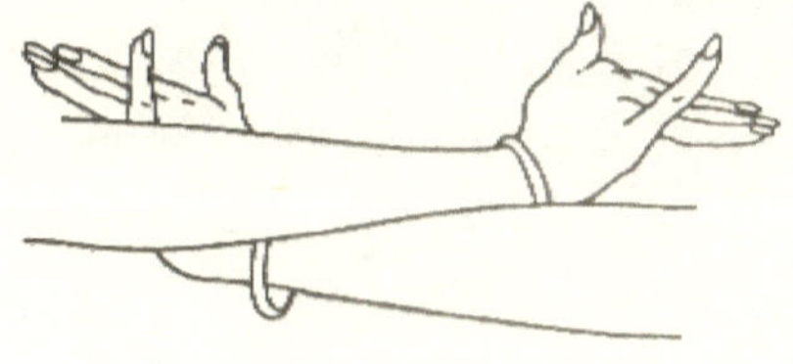

Meanings:

Agalingana   - To embrace somebody

Lajyaa   - Shyness

Angadaadi-Pradarshana   - To show a body

Baalaanaam-shikshana - Nursing a baby

(8) Shivalinga hasta Viniyogaha

Viniyogasthu Thasyeiva

Shivalingasya Darshanay

Meanings:

Shivalingasya Darshana - To denote 

                       Shivalingam

(9) Katakaavardhana hasta Viniyogaha

Patttabhishekay Poojaayaam

Vivaahaadishu Yujyathay

Meanings:

Patttabhisheka   - Coronation

Poojaa   - To do pooja

Vivaaha   - Marriage

(10) Karthari-swasthika hasta Viniyogaha

Shaakaashu Cha Aadrishikaray Vruksheshu cha Niyujyathay

Meanings:

Shaakaa — - Branch

Aadrishikara — - Hill top or summit

Vruksha — - Tree

(11) Shakata hasta Viniyogaha

Raakshsa-abhinayeh Praayaha Shakatoo

Viniyujyathay

Meaning:

Raakshsa-abinaya - To show a demon

(12) Shank hasta Viniyogaha

Shankaadishu Prayojyoyaa Mithyaahur

Bharathaadayaha

Meaning:

Shanka - To denote the usage of conch

(13) Chakra hasta Viniyogaha

Chakrahasta Cha Vinayehyascha

Charaarthay Viniyujyatha

Meaning:

Chakra - To denote a wheel

(14) Samputa hasta Viniyogaha

Vasthavaachaaday Samputaycha Samputa kara Yeerithatha

Meanings:

Vasthvaachada -   To cover things

Samputa -   Respresenting a box

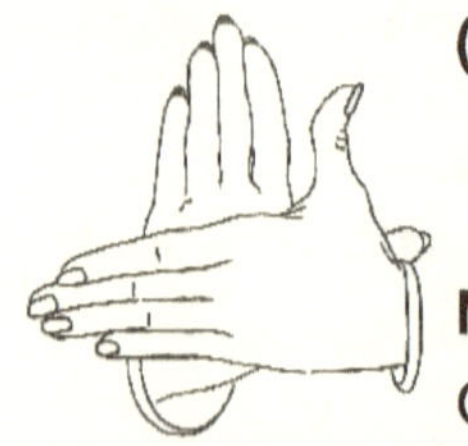

(15) Paashaa hasta Viniyogaha

Anyonyakalahay Paashey Srunkalaayaam Niyujyathay

Meanings:

Anyonyakalaha - Fighting with each-other (between lovers)

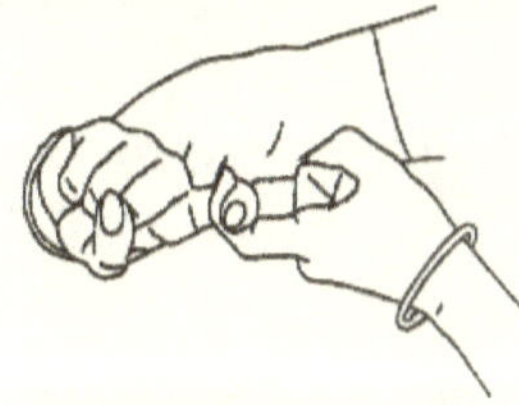

Paasha	-	A rope
Srunkalaaya	-	A chain

(16) Keelakav hasta Viniyogaha

Sneheh Narmaanulaapaycha keelakav Viniyujyathay

Meanings:

Sneheh   - Affection (love)

Narmaanulaapa - Talking with each other
                         (when in love)

(17) Mastya hasta viniyogaha

Yehthasya Vinyogasthu Sammatho Mastya Darshanay

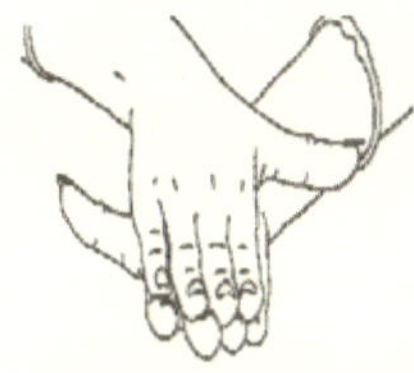

Meaning:

Matsya Darshana - To denote a fish

(18) Koorma hasta Viniyogaha

Koorma hasta Cha Vigneyyah

Koormaarthay Viniyujyathay

Meaning:

Koorma - To denote a tortoise

(19) Varaaha hasta Viniyogaha

Yehthasya Viniyogaha Syaadvaraahartha Pradarshanay

Meaning:

Varaaha - To denote a Wild Pig (or) Boar

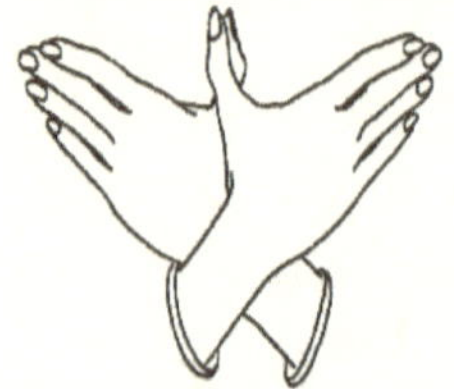

(20) Garuda hasta Viniyogaha

Garudahasthacha Yithyaahur Garudaarthay Viniyujyathay

Meaning:

Garuda - To denote an eagle (Garudan)

(21) Naagabhanda hasta Viniyogaha

Yehthasya Viniyogasthu Naagabhanday
Hee Sammathaha

Meaning:

Naagabhandha - To denote two snakes together

(22) Katvaa hasta Viniyogaha

Katvaahastoo Bhaveydesha Katvaa-
Shivikayoo Smruthaha

Meaning:

Katvaa - To denote a cot

(23) Berundaka hasta Viniyogaha

Bhehrundo Pakshi-dhumbhathyoo
Berundo Yujyathay Karaha

Meanings:

Bhehrunda - To denote Behrundaka bird

Pakshi-dhumbathyo -   A pair of birds

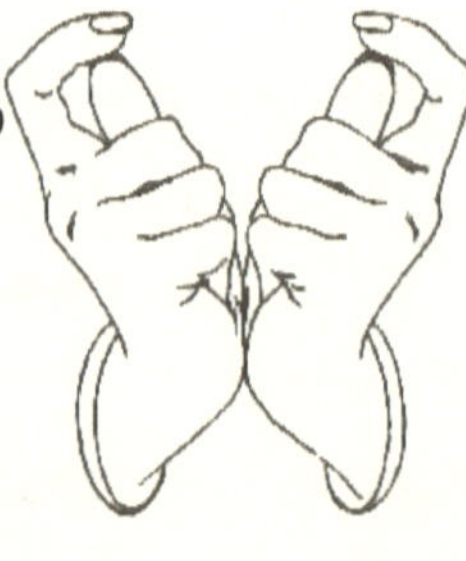

DESAVATHARAHASTHA

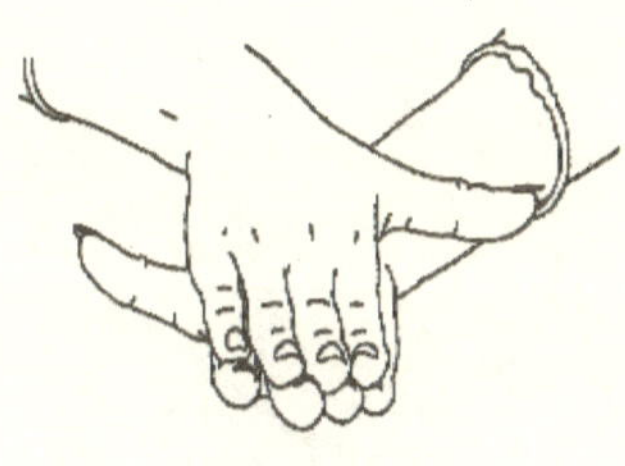

Matsya

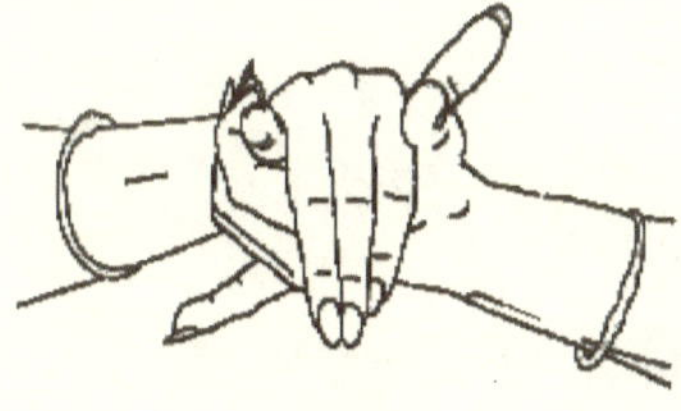

Koorma

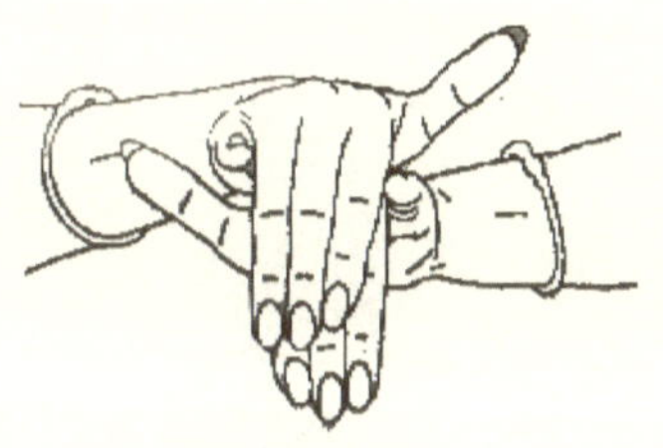

Varaha

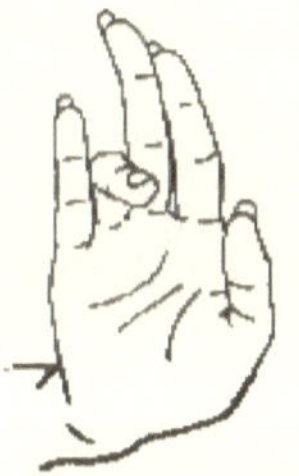

Narasimha

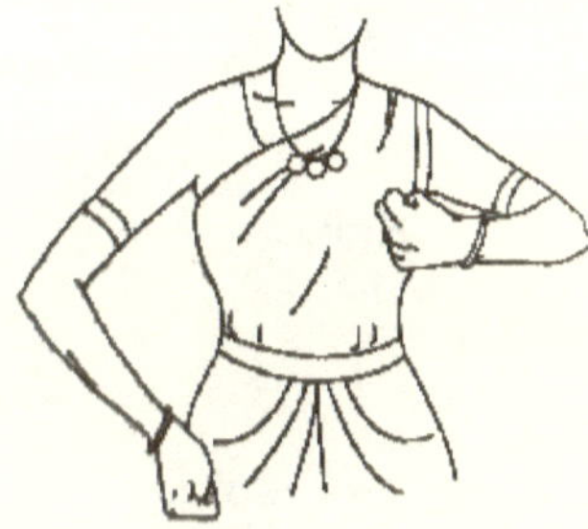

Vamana

Parashurama

SreeRama

Balarama

Krishna

Kalki

DEVA HASTAS

Name	Right	Left
Brahma	Hamsasyo	Chaturam
Vishnu	Thripathakam	Thripathakam
Shiva	Thripathakam	Simhamukam
Saraswathi	Soochi	Kapitham
Lakshmi	Kapitham	Kapitham
Parvathi	Pathakam	Pathakam
Ganapathi	Kapitham	Kapitham
Muruga	Shikaram	Trishulam
Manmatha	Katakamukam	Shikaram
Indra	Thripathakam	Thripathakam
Varuna	Pathakam	Shikaram
Vayu	Aralam	Ardhapathakam
Agni	Tripathakam	Kangoolam
Kubera	Mushti	Alapadmam
Nirdhi	Shakatam	Katva
Yama	Soochi	Thaamrachootam

Brahma

Vishnu

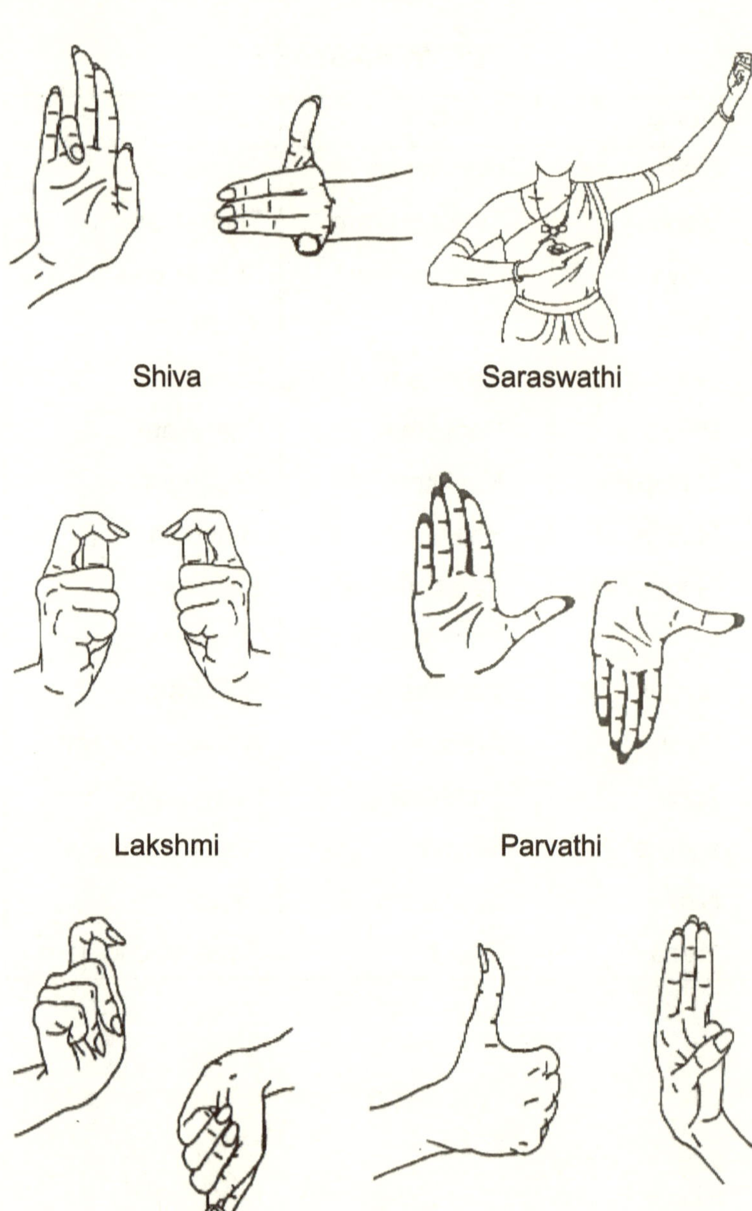

Shiva
Saraswathi
Lakshmi
Parvathi
Ganapathi
Muruga

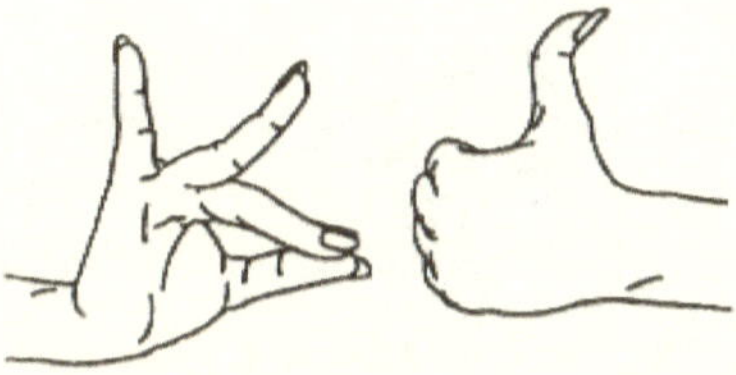

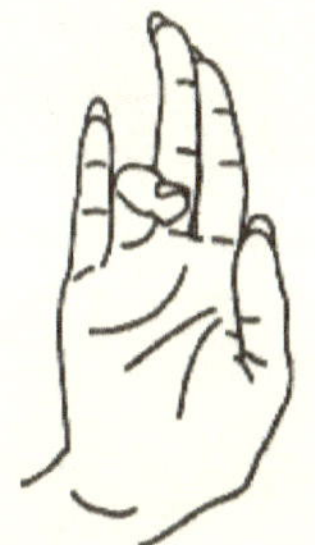

Manmatha

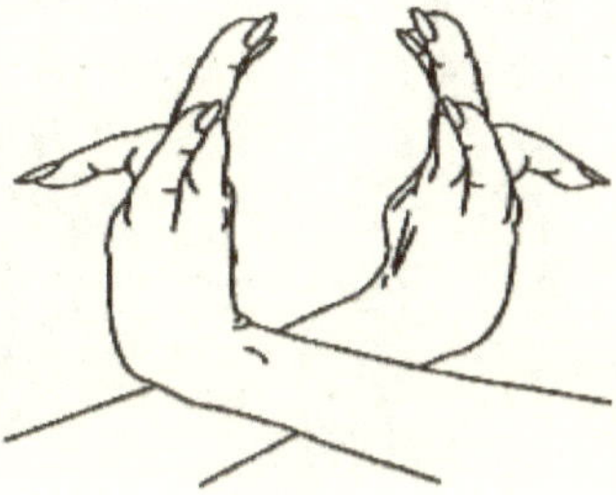

Indra

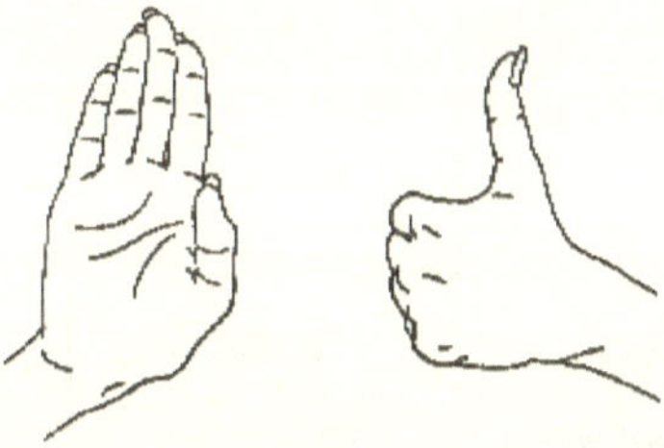

Varuna

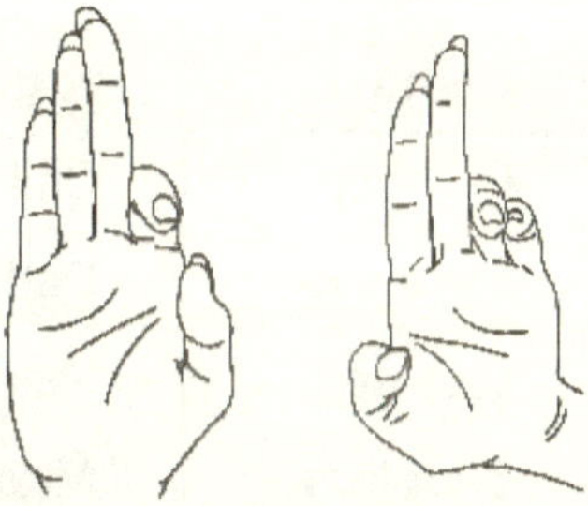

Vayu

Agni

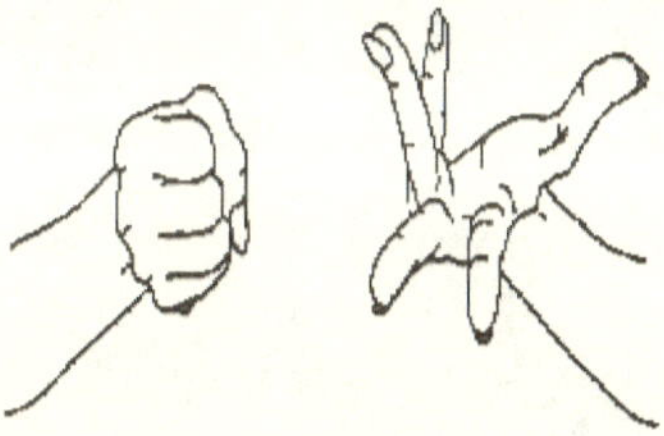

Kubera

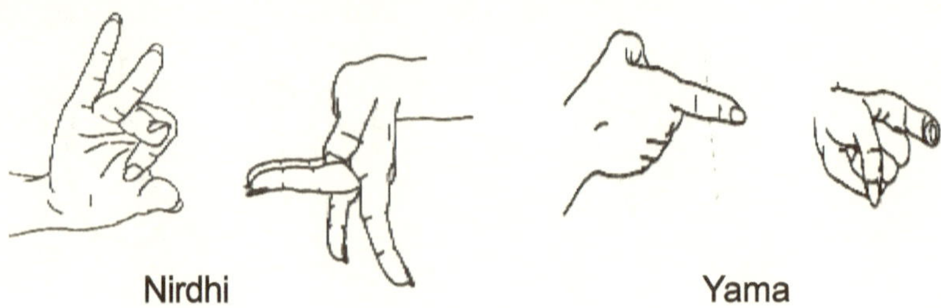

Nirdhi   Yama

JATHI HASTAS

Name	Right	Left
Brahmin	Shikaram	Shikaram
Shathriya	Pathakam	Shikaram
Vaishya	Katakamukam	Hamsasyo
Shoothra	Mrugasheersham	Shikaram
Rakshasha	Shakatam	Shakatam

Brahmin   Shathriya   Vaishya

Shoothra   Rakshasha

BANDAVA HASTAS

Name	Right	Left
Husband & Wife	Mrugasheersha	Shikaram
Mother	Mukula - Alapadmam	Ardhachandran
Father	Shikaram	Mukula-Alapadmam
Mother-in-law	Sandamsa	Hamsasya
Father-in-law	Shikaram	Hamsasya
Daughter	Alapadmam	Mrugasheersham
Son	Alapadmam	Shikaram
Daughter-in-law	Mrugasheersham	Shikaram
Sister-in-law	Mrugasheersham	Shikaram
Brother-in-law	Karthari	Shikaram
Brother	Mayuram	Shikaram
Co-wives	Mrugasheersha	Mrugasheersha

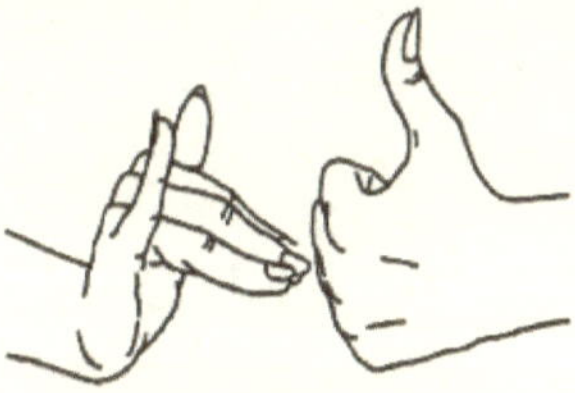

Husband & Wife

Mother

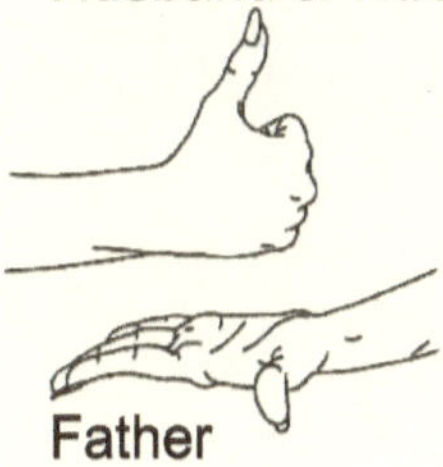

Father

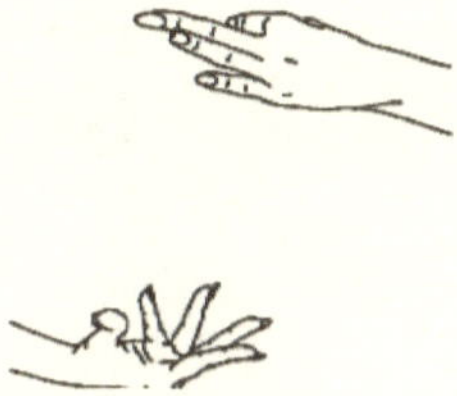

Mother-in-law

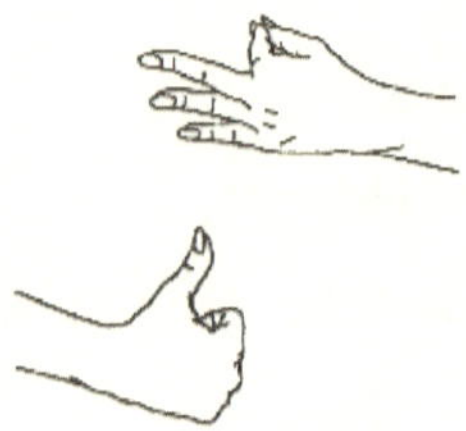

Father-in-law

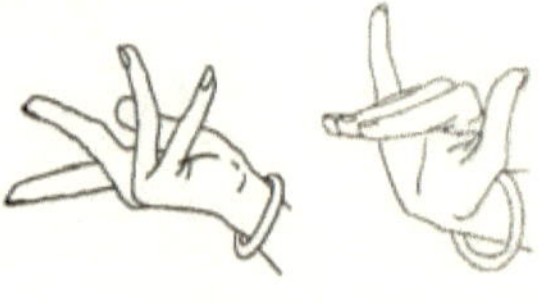

Daughter

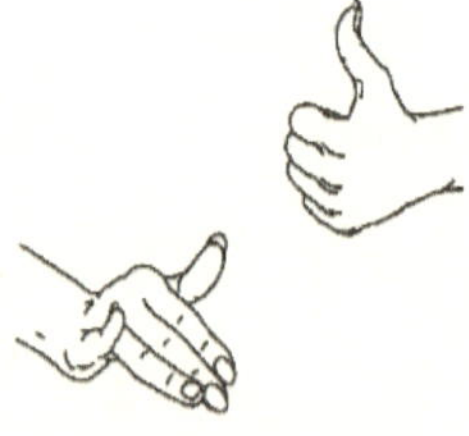

Son

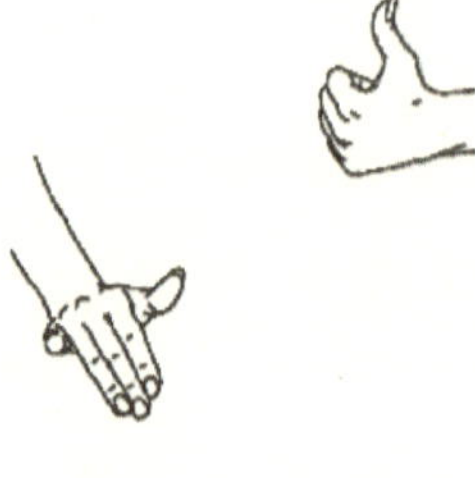

Daughter-in-law

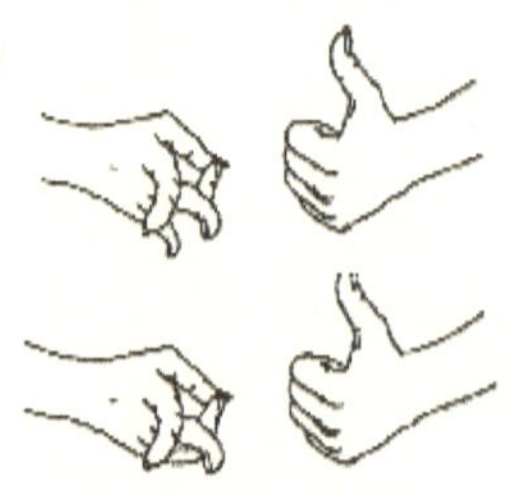

Sister-in-law

Brother-in-law

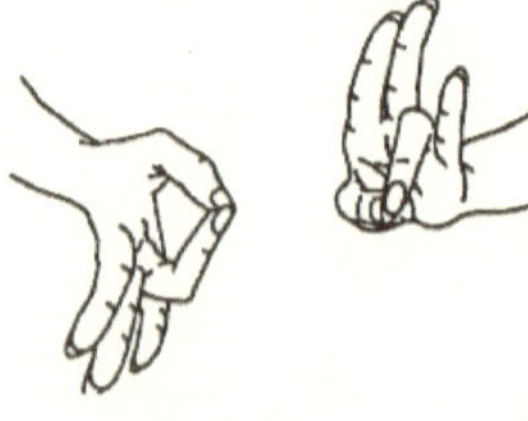

Brother

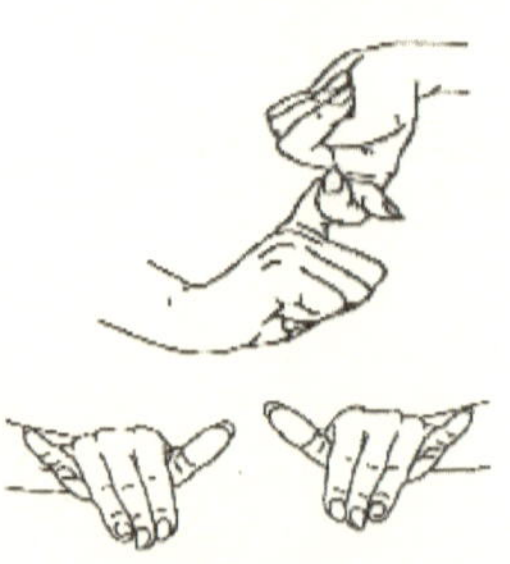

Co-wives

NAVAGRAHA HASTAS

Name	Right	Left
Surya (Sun)	Kapitham	Alapadmam
Chandra (Moon)	Pathakam	Alapadmam
Kucha (Mars)	Mushti	Soochi
Budha (Mercury)	Pathakam	Shikaram
Guru (Jupiter)	Shikaram	Shikaram
Shukra (Venus)	Mushti	Mushti
Shani (Saturn)	Trishulam	Shikaram
Raghu	Soochi	Sarpasheersham
Kethu	Pathakam	Soochi

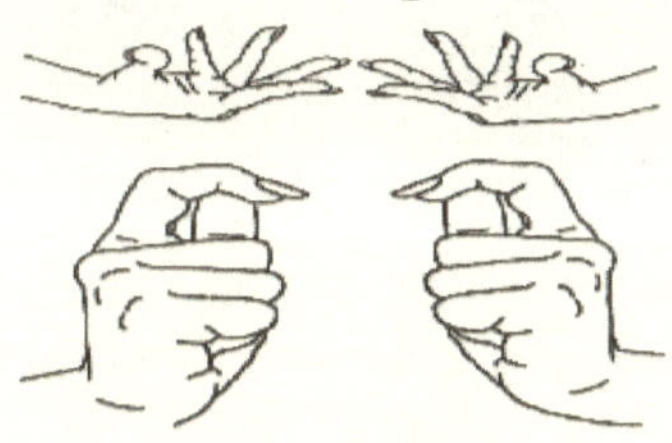

Surya

Chandra

Kucha

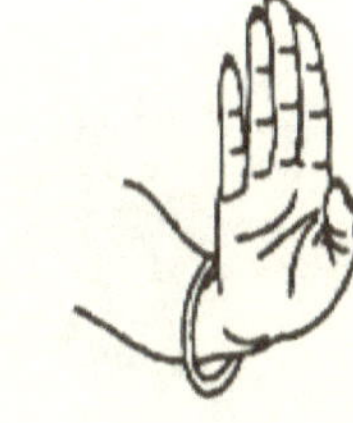

Budha

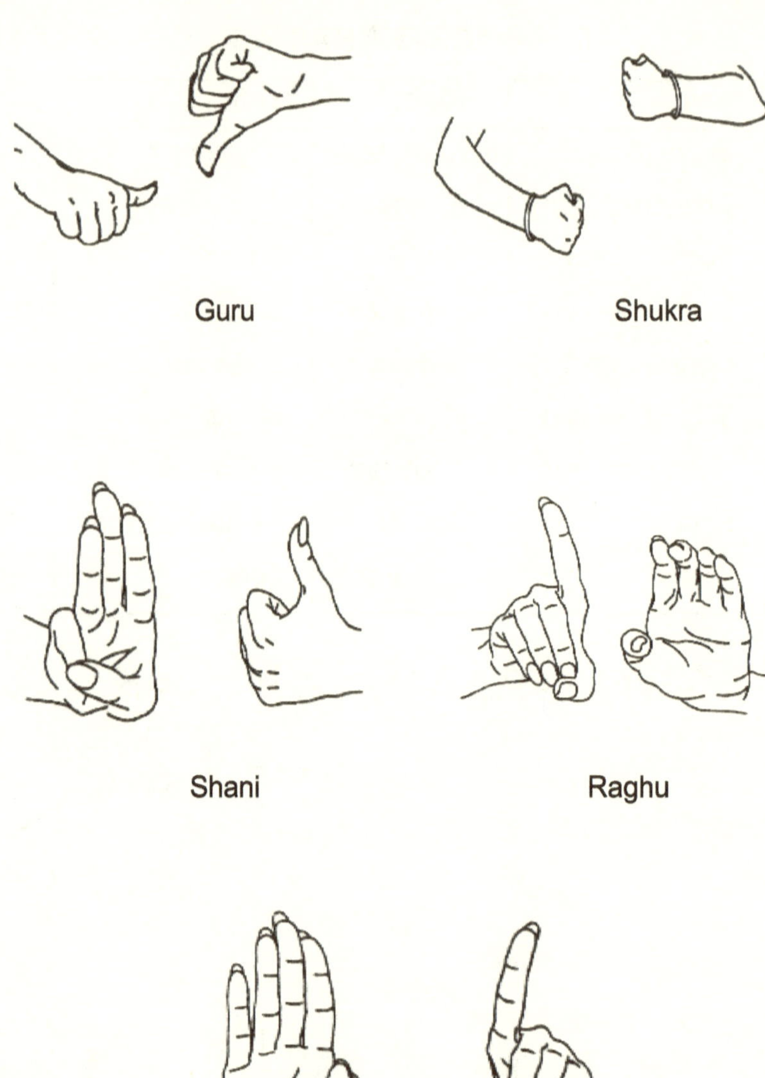

Guru

Shukra

Shani

Raghu

Kethu

SHIRO BHEDA VINIYOGHA
(Head Movements)

Samam Udhvaahitham Adhomukam Aalolitham Dhutham

Kampitamcha Paraavurththam Ukshiptham Parivaahitham

Navadaakathitham-sheersham Naatyashaastra-Vishaaradeihee

Meanings:

Samam	- To be straight
Udhvaahitham	- To move up
Adhomukam	- To move down
Aalolitham	- To move around
Dhutham	- To move it from side to side
Kampitam	- To move it up and down
Paraavurththam	- To turn the face
Ukshiptham	- To turn the head from one side to other side and to lift
Paraavurththam	- To say Can't

(1) Sama Shira Viniyogaha

Naatyarambhay Japaadavcha Garvay Pranayakopayoho

Sthambhay Nishkriyathvaycha Samasheersha Mudhaahrutham

Meanings:

Naatyarambhay	- Beginning of dance
Japaadavcha	- While in Meditation
Garva	- Pride
Pranayakopa	- Pretend anger of love
Sthambha	- Surprise (or) Astonishment
Nishkriyathvaycha	- In response when not doinganything

(2) Udhvaahitha Shira Viniyogaha

Dwajay Chandray cha Gaganay Parvathay Vyoomagaamishu

Thungavasthuni Samyooj-Mudhvaahitha Shiro-Vidhuhu

Meanings:

Dwaja	- Flag
Chandra	- Moon
Gagana	- Sky
Parvatha	- Mountain
Vyomagaamishu	- Flying objects (birds)
Thungavasthu	- Very high objects (tower, hills, etc)

(3) Adhomuka Shira Viniyogaha

Lajja Kayday Pranaameshu Duschinthaa Moorchayosthathaa

Adah-Sthithaartha-nirdeshey Yujyathay-ambhuni Mujjanay

Meanings:

Lajjaa	- Shyness
Kayda	- Sorrow
Pranaama	- Bowing elders
Duschinthaa	- Evil thoughts
Moorcha	- Fainting
Adah-Sthithaartha-nirdesha	- Things placed below
Ambhunimujja	- Plunge into water

(4) Aalolitha Shira Viniyogaha

Nidrodwega-Grahaaveyshey Madha-Moorchaasu Thanmatham

Brahmanay Vikato-dhaamahasyeh Chaalolitham Shiraha

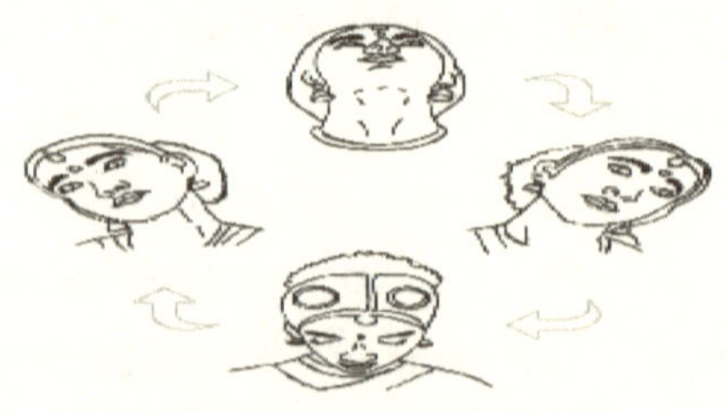

Meanings:

Nidrodwega	- To denote sleepyness
Grahaaveysha	- Position by an evil spirit
Madha	- Ego
Moorchasa	- To faint
Unmatham	- In-toxication
Brahmana	- Rotation (or) travelling
Vikato-dhaamahasya	- Uncontrollable laughter

(5) Dhutha Shira viniyogaha

Naastheethivachanay-bhooyaha Paarshva-deshaavalokanay

Janaavaasay Vismayehcha Vishaaday-Anipsithay Thathaa

Sheethaarthay Jwarithay Bheethay Sadhyah-peethaasavay Thathaa

Yudhey Yanthray Nisheydaadava-marshey Swaangaveekshanay

Paarshvaahanay Thasyokthaha Prayogo Bharathaadibihee

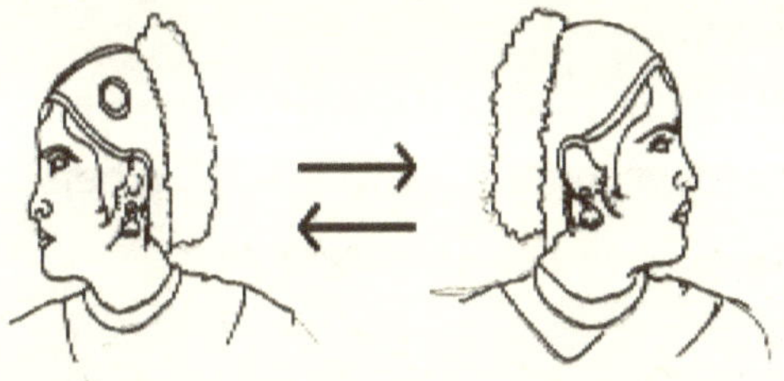

Meanings:

Naastheethivachanay-bhooyaha	-	Saying "I don't know"
Paarshva-deshaavalokana	-	Looking to the sides
Janaavaasa	-	Discussing with others
Vismaya	-	Astonishment
Vishaada	-	Sadness
Anipsitha	-	Unwillingness
Sheethaartha	-	Effects of cold
Jwara	-	Fever

Bheetha	-	Fear
Sadhyah-peethaasa	-	Drinking liquor
Yudha	-	Battle
Yanthra	-	Effort to carry things
Nisheydaadava-marsha	-	Refusing agitation
Swaangaveekshana	-	Glancing at their own limbs
Paarshvaahana	-	Calling from the sides

(6) Kampitha Shira Viniyogaha

Roshey Thishtaythi-vachanay Prashnay Sankyopa-huthayoho

Avaahanav Tharjanav Cha Kampitham vinivuivathay

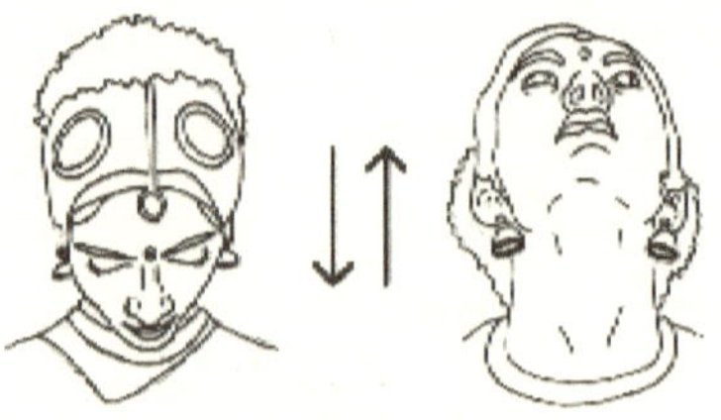

Meanings:

Rosha	- Anger
Thishtaythi-vachana	- To say "stop here"
Prashna	- Questioning
Sankyopa	- Counting
Avaahana	- Inviting the deities
Tharjana	- Threatening

(7) Paraavrutha Shira Viniyogaha

Thathakaaryam Kopa-Lajjaadikruthay Vakthaprasaaranay

Anaadaray Kachey Thoonyaam Paraavruthashiro-vidhuhu

Meanings:

Thathakaaryam	- Commanding
Kopa	- Anger
Lajja	- Shyness

Vakthaprasaarana - Turning away the face

Anaadara — - Slighting

Kacha — - Catching the hair

Thoonyaa — - Quiver (Container used to carry arrows)

(8) Ukshiptha Shira Viniyogaha

Gruhanaa-gacheythyaa-dhayarthasoochanay Pariposhanay

Angikkaray Prayokthavyam Parivaahitha Sheershakam

Meanings:

Gruha — - Gacheythyaa

Pariposhana — - Supporting

Angikkara — - Acceptation

Dhayarthasoochan - To command (or) request

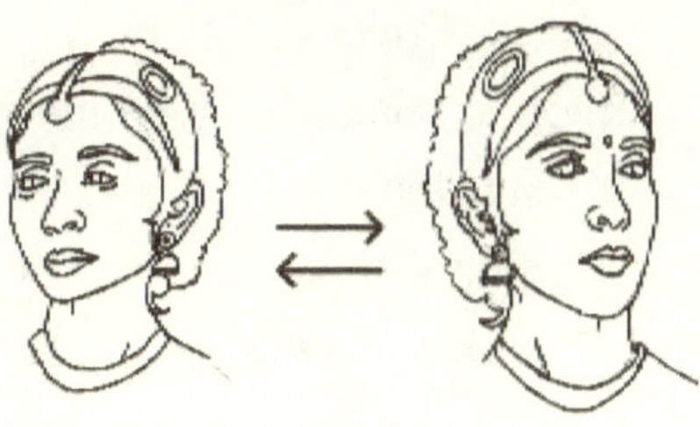

(9) Parivaahitha Shira Viniyogaha

Mohay Cha Viraheh Sthoothray Santhooshey Chaanumodhanay

Vichaaray Cha Prayokthvyam Parivaahitha Sheershakam

Meanings:

Moha — - Infactuation

Viraha — - Longing for the separated love

Sthothra — - Praising the dities

Santhosha — - Happiness

Anumodha — - Approval

Vichaara — - Thinking in grief (deep sorrow)

DRUSHTI BHEDA VINIYOGAHA
(Eye Movements)

Samam Aalookitham Saachi Praalokitha Nimeelithay

Ulokitha Anuvrutheycha Thataacheivaavalokitham

Meanings:

Samam	-	To look straight
Aalookitham	-	To look around
Saachi	-	To look to oneside
Praalokitha	-	Looking on both the sides
Nimeelitha	-	Half closing
Ulokitha	-	To look up
Anuvrutha	-	To look up and down
Avalokitham	-	To look down (at a distance)

(1) Sama Drushti Viniyogaha

Naatyaarambhey Thulaayaamcha Chaapyanya-chintaa-vinishchayeh

Aashcharyeh Devathaaroopay Samadrushti-Rudhaahruthaa

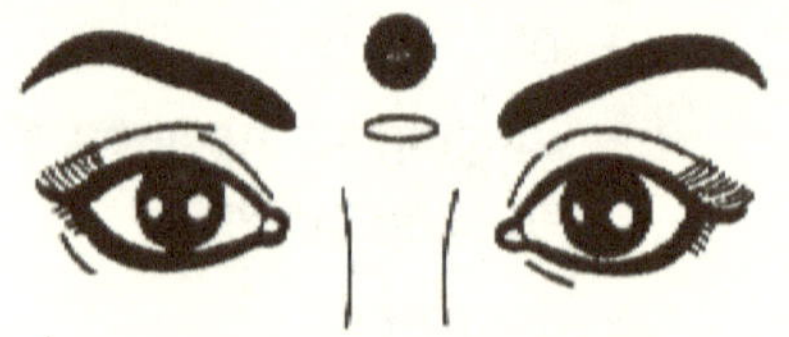

Meanings:

Naatyaarambha	-	Beginning of dance
Thulaayaam	-	Scale (Physical balance)
Anyanyachintaa	-	Effort to think what the other person is thinking
Aashcharya	-	Surprisre
Devathaaroopa	-	To look at the image of God

(2) Aalokitha Drushti Viniyogaha

Kulaalachakra-bramaneh Sarva-vasthu-Pradarshanay

Yaachnyanyaamcha Prayokthavyam Aalokitha-Nireekshanam

Meanings:

Kulaalachakrabramana - Circular movements of potter's wheel

Sarvavasthu Pradarshana - To show all the things

Yaachnyanyaam   - Begging

(3) Saachi Drushti Viniyogaha

Ingithey Shamshru- sparshey Sharalakshyeh Shukay Smuruthav

Soochanaayaam Cha Kaaryaanam Naatyeh-saachi-nireekshanam

Meanings:

Ingitha	- Look to the side (denotes hinting)
Shamshru- sparshey	- To touch the moustache
Sharalakshya	- Drawing an arrow
Shuka Smuruthav	- Parrot
Soochanaayaam	- To point out the Karyaanam
	Remembrance of the past
Naatya	- Dance

(4) Praalokitha Drushti Viniyogaha

Ubhayoho Paarshvayorvasthu Nirdeshyeh cha Prasamjithey

Chalanay Budhijaatyeh Cha Praalokitha-nireekshnam

Meanings :

Ubhayoho Paarshvayorvasthu Nirdeshya	- It is used to denote things situated on both the sides
Prasamjitha	- Happiness
Chalana	- Moving
Bhudhijaatya	- Idiocy (idiotic condition)

(5) Nimeelitha Drushti Viniyogaha

Aasheevisheh Paaravasheyeh Japay Dhyaney Namaskruthav

Ummaadhey Sookshmadrushtavcha Cha Nimeelithaa Drushti-reerithaa

Meanings :

Aasheevisha	- Showing snake
Paaravasheya	- Being under another man's power
Japa	- Prayer

Dhyana	- Meditation
Namaskrutham	- Salute
Ummaadha	- Madness
Sookshmadrushti	- Keen observation

(6) Ulokitha Drushti Viniyogaha

Dwajaagrey Gopurey Devamandalay Poorvajanmanee

Avunnathyeh Chandrikadhaava-Ullokitha Nireekshanam

Meanings :

Dwajaagra	- Flag (top of the flag)
Gopura	- Temple Tower
Devamandala	- Heavens
Poorvajanma	- Previous birth
Auvnathya	- Places of height
Chandrika	- Moonlight

(7) Anuvrittha Drushti Viniyogaha

Kopadrushotu Priyamanthrey Anuvrittha Nireekshnam

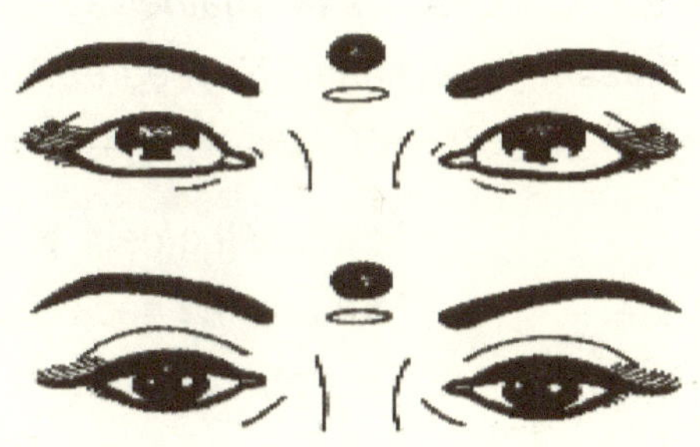

Meanings :

Kopadrushti	- Angrily look
Priyamanthra	- Calling with affection

(8) Avalokitha Drushti Viniyogaha

Chayalokay Vicharey Chayaryaam Patanashrameh
Swaangaavalookanay Yaanay Avalokithmuchyathey

Meanings :

Chayaloka	- Looking at the shadow
Vichara	- Reflection
Charya	- To do exercise
Patana	- Effort to study
Shramaa	- Fatigue
Swaangavalokana	- Looking at one's own limbs

GREEVA BHEDHA VINIYOGAHA

Sundareecha Tirascheena Thatheivaparivarthithaa
Praakampithaacha Bhavagneh Neyaagreevaa Chathurvida

Meanings :

Sundaree	- To move the neck to the sides
Thirascheenaa	- To move the neck to the sides in a serpentive fashion

Parivarthithaa - To do circular movements with theneck

Praakampithaacha Bhavagneh - To move the neck

in front and back

(1) Sundaaree Greeva Viniyogaha

Sneyhaarambhey Thathaayathney Samyagarthey cha Visthruthay

Sarasthvaanumodhey cha saa Greevaa Sundaree Mathaa

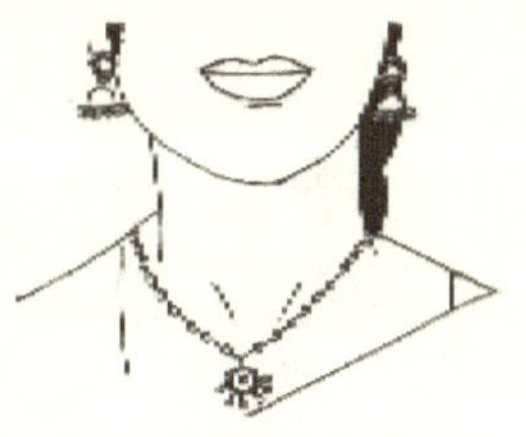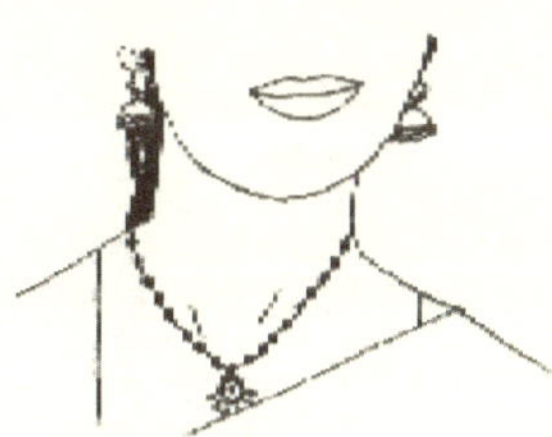

Meanings :

Sneyharambha	- Beginning of affection
Yathna	- Effor
Samayagartha	- Fulfilment
Visthrutha	- Width
Sarasthvaanumodha	- Approval with pleasure

(2) Thirascheenaa Greeva Viniyogaha

Kadgashramay Sarpagathyaam Thirascheenaa Prayujyathey

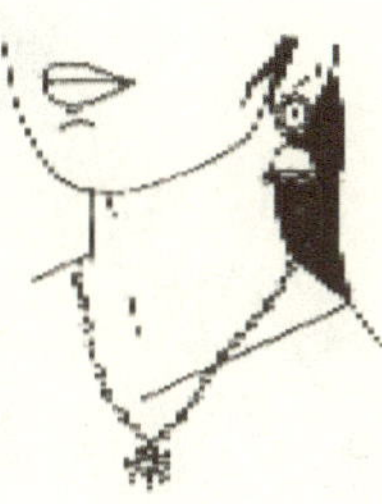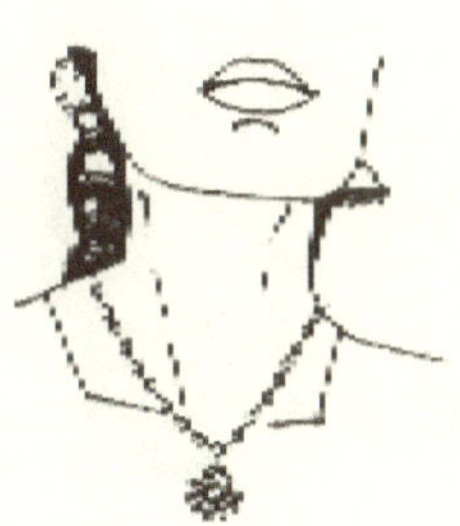

Meanings :

Kadgashrama	- Exercise with sword
Sarpagahtya	- Gliding movements of snake

(3) Parivartha Greevaa Viniyogaha

Sringaaranataneh Kaanthakapola-dwayachumbahnay

Naatyathanthra-vichaaragnaihee prayojyaa Parivarthithaa

Meanings :

Sringaaranatana - Graceful movements of dance Kaantha

Kapola - To kiss both the cheeks of the beloved

Dwayachumbahna - Those who knows the secret of the dance

Naatyathanthra - Vichaaragna

(4) Praakampitha Greeva Viniyogaha

Yushmadhasmaadhithi Prokkthey Desheenaatyeh Visheshathaha

Dholaayaam Manithey Cheiva Prayokthavyaa Praakampithaa

Meanings :

Yushmadasmaadhithi Prokktha - Telling "you and I"

Deshsheenaatya   - Folk dance

Vishesha   - To explain the qualities

Dholaa   - Swinging

Manitha   - Murmuring sound of a women in condigual happiness

PAADABHEDA

Vakshyathe paadha bhedaanam lakshanam poorva sammatham

Mandala-uthplavane chaiva bhramari paadhacharika

Chathurdha paadhabhedas syuh thesham lakshanam uchyathe

Leg movements or positioning of the feet. Now the types of positions of feet (in dance) are set out with a definitions.that have been approved earlier .They are four in number.

Mandala (Standing posture)

Uthplavana (Jumping)

Bhramaree (fight movement)

Paadhacharee(Graceful gate)

Mandalabhedhaah

Sthaanakam chaaayathaaleedam prenkhana prerithaani cha

Prathyaleedam swasthikascha motitham samasoochika

Paarswasoocheethi cha dasha mandalani eerithaaneeha The mandala(standing posture)has ten varieties. They are sthaanaka, aayatha, aaleeda, prathyaleeda, prenkhana, preritha, svasthika, motitha,samasoochee, paarswasoochee.

Sthaanaka mandalam:

Katim sprshtvaa ardhachandraakhya paanibhyam samapaadathah

Samarekhathayaa thishteth thath syath sthaanaka

Mandalam Touching the hip with ardhachandra hands and standing with feet together in the same line is called Sthaanaka mandalam.

Aayathamandalam

Vithasthi antharithau paadhau krithvaa thu chathurshrakau

Thiryak kunchitha jaanubhaayam sthithir aayathamandalam

Standing on both feet with half the normal distance apart between each little is aayathamandalam.

Aaleedam:

Dashinaanghreshcha purathah vithasthi thrithayaantharam

Vinyaseth vaamapaadamcha shikharam vaamapaaninaa

Katakamughahasthashcha dakshinena dhrutho yadi

Aaleedamandalamithi vikhyatham bharathaadibhih.

Extending the left foot in front of the right one at one-and-a- half length (one length is anapproximate measurement-normally, the distance from elbow to the tip of the middle finger), showing shikhara with the left hand and katakaamugha with right hand-this posture is called Aaleeda according to Bharatha and others.

Prathyaaleedam

Aaleedasya viparyaasaath

prathyaaleedaakhya mandalam

The reverse(with respect to the right and left of hands and feet respectively).

Prenkhanam

Prasrthya ekapadam paarshve

paarshnideshasya paadathah

Sthitvaanthe korma hasthena sthithih

prenkhana mandalam

Placing one foot by the side of another and showing Koorma gesture through the hands,the prenkhana mandala is achieved.

Preritham

Santhaadya ekam paadam paarshve vithasthi thrithayaantharam

Thiryak kunjitha jaanubhyam sthithvaa atha shikaram karam

Vidhaaya vakshasi anyena prasrtha cha pathakikaa

Pradardshayeth idham thajjnaah preritham mandalam vidhuu.

Bringing one foot to the front with thud(on earth) at a distance of one and a half lengths and standing with knees bent and placed across each other while showing the shikara and on the chest and showing the pathaka gesture through the other hand that is extended – This is called Prerithamandala.

Svasthikam

Dakshinoththarathah kuryaath Padhee padam kare karam

Vyathyaasena thadha proktham svasthikam naama mandalam

When the right foot and left foot are placed across each other and if the two hands are also kept across each other ,then it is called Svasthikamandala.

Motitham

Prapadhaabhyaam bhuvi sthithva jaanuyugmena samsprsheth

Kramaath bhoothalam ekaikam thripataaka karadhvayam

Krthvaa thanmotitham naama mandalam kathitham bhudhaih

Sitting on the raised heel,feet flexed and with toes raised and touching the ground with each knee alternately,and the same time making thipathaaka with both the hands,the Motitha mandala is made.

Samasoochi

Paadhaagraabhyaam cha jaanubhyam bhoothalam samsprshed yadhi
Mandalam samasoocheethi kathitham poorva

When both the feet and the knees touch
the ground, it is called samasoochi
mandala according to ancient masters.

Paarsvasoochi

Sthithva paadhaagrayugmena jaanunaa ekena paarsvatnan
Samsprsheth bhoothalam paarsvasoochi mandalameeritham

Sitting on the raised heel with feet flexed
and touching the ground with just one knee,
the gesture shown is paasvasoochi.

STHAANAKABHEDHAAH

Paadha vinyasabhedena
Sthaanakam Shadvidham matham
Samapaadham cha ekapaadham naagaban
dhas thathah param aindram cha gaarudam chaiva,
brahmasThaanam ithi kramaath

Resting Postures

According to the positioning of the feet, th resting postures are
six in number samapaadha, Ekapaadha, Naagabandh Aindhra,
Gaaruda and Brahma.

Samapaadhasthaanam

Sthithih samaabhyaam paadhabhyaam samapaadham ithi smrtham

Pushpaanjalau dhevaroope samapaadham niyujyathe

The positioning of both the feet equally without tilting on either side) is called samapaadha. It is employed in pushpaanjali offering of flowers) and in the posture representing gods.

Ekapaadhasthanam

Jaanvaashrithya padhaikena Sthithi ssyaatheka paaanakam

Ekapaadham thu idham sthanam nishchale thapasi sthitham

Standing on one foot and placing the other across the knee of that foot is called 'ekapaadha'. It is employed while denoting standing still and penance.

Naagabandhasthaanam

Paadham paadhena samveshtya thathaa paanim cha paaninaasthithis syaath

naagaban Dhaakhyaa naagabandhe prayujyathe

The position attained by twisting one foot with the other and one hand with the other is called 'naagabandha'. It is used for denoting intertwining of serpents.

Aindrakasthaanam

Paadham ekam samaakunchya
Sthithvaa anyapadha jaanunee
Uththaanithe karam nyasyas
Thithir aindhram itheeritham.
Vaasave raajabhaave cha
Sthaanam aindhram niyujyathe

The position of standing with one leg be
he other leg and knee raised up and the har
being held freely is called 'Aindhra' posture.
It is used for indicating Indra or a King.

Garudasthaanakam

Aaleeda mandale pashchaath
atha jaanuthalam bhuvi
Samsthapya paa niyugmena
vahan viralamandalam
vaamam aakunchitham
krthvaa thadhanyam jaanunaa bhuvi
niveshayeth prshta bhaage
sthaanakam gaarudam bhaveth

In the 'aaleeda mandala' posture, if one knee is placed on the ground and the hands show the gesture (required) it is called gadudasthaanaka

Brahmasthaanam

Jaanoopari padham nyasya
Padhasyopari jaanu cha
Sthitham yadhi bhaveth braamham
Japaadishu niyujyathe

Placing one foot on one knee and another foot on the other knee, the Brahma posture is shown. It is employed for indicating meditation.

GATHIBHEDHAAH:

Athaathra gathibhedaanam
lakshanam vakshyathe kramaath
hamsee mayooree cha mrgee gajaleelaa thurangi
Nee suimhee bhujangee mandookee
gathir veeraa cha maanaveedashaithaa gathayo jneyaa
naatya shaastra vishaaradhaih

Gathibhedhaah (Types of stepping)

Then the definitions of ten kinds of stepping are given respectively, according to the experts in the science of dance. They are: Hamsee (Goose step) Mayooree (Peacock step), mrgee (deer step), gajaleela (elephant step), thuranginee (horse step), simbhee (lion step), bhujangee (snake step), mandookee (frog step), veeraa (heroic step) and maanavee (human step).

HAMSEEGATHIH

Vithasthyantharitham shanaih
Ekaikam thath padham nyasya
Kapiththam karayorvahan hamsavadhgamanam
Yaththu saa hamseegathireerithaa.

The Goose step

Turning the body sideways, placing one foot after another at a distance of one length, showing kapiththa with both the hands, stepping like a goose is called Goose step.

MAYOOREEGATHIH

Prapadhaabhyaam bhuvi sthithvaa
Kapiththam karayorvahan
Ekaikajaanuchalanaath mayooree gathireeyathe

The Peacock step

Standing on toes on the ground and showing Kapiththa with both the hands and moving on the knees one after the other, is called the peacock step.

MRGEEGATHIH

Mrgavadh gamanam vegaath thripathaakakarau vahan
Purathah paarshvayoshchaiva yaanam mrgagathirbhavet

The Deer step

Moving quickly forward and sideways like a deer, showing Tripathaaka hand is called the deer step.

GAJALEELAAGATHIH

Paarshvayosthu pathaakaabhyaam
Karaabhyaam vicharamsthathah samapaadhagathir mandham
Gajaleelethi vishruthaa.

The Elephant step

Walking slowly with equal feet (without tilting on eitherside) and holding pathaakaa on both sides is said to be the elephant step.

THURANGINEEGATHIH

UthkShipya dakshinam paadham
Ullangya cha muhurmuhuh
Vaamena shikharam Dhrthvaa
Dhakshinena pathaakikaam thuranginee gathih prokthaa
Nrththashaahstra vishaaradhaih

The Horse step

Raising the right foot and jumping again and again, bearing Shikhara on the left hand and Pathaaka on the right hand is called the horse step, according to the experts of the science of dance.

SIMHEEGATHIH

Paadhaagraabhyaam bhuvi sthithvaa
Pura uthpluthya vegathah karaabhyaam shikharam
Dhrthvaa yaanam simheegathir bhaveth

The Lion step

Standing steadily on toes and jumping swiftly and marching forward, bearing shikhara in both the hands is called the lion step.

BHUJANGEEGATHI

Thripathaakakarau Dhrthvaa
Paarshvayorubhayorapi,
Poorvavadhgamanam yaththu
Saa bhujangee gathir bhaveth.

The Snake step

Bearing Tripathaaka in both the hands and walking as before is called the snake step.

MANDOOKEEGATHIH

Karaabhyaam shikharam Dhrthvaa
Kinchith simheesamaa gathih
Mandookee gathirithyeshaa
prasidhdhaa bharathaagame

The Frog step

Showing shikhara in both the hands and moving a bit like the lion step is popularly known as the frog step in the science of Bharatha.

VEERAAGATHIH

Vaame thu shikharam dhrthvaa
DhakshiNena pathaakikaa dhooraadhaagamanam
Yaththu veeraa gathiritheerithaa.

The heroic step

Showing the Shikhara on the left hand and Pathaka on the right from the rear (or corners) is called the heroic step.

MANAVEEGATHIH

Mandalaakaaravath bhraanthyaa
samaagathya muhurmuhuh
vaamam karam nyasya katau
dhakshine katakaamukham manavee
gathirithyeshaa prasidhdhaa poorvasooribih.

The Human step

Coming again and again in circles (Mandala) as though out of delusion, keeping the left hand on the hip and showing katakaamukha with the right is popularly called as the human step according to the ancient experts.

BHARATHANATYAM: THE ETERNAL DANCE

Bharathanatyam, a timeless treasure of India's cultural heritage, is more than just a dance form. It is a sacred journey that weaves together art, spirituality, and tradition into a mesmerizing tapestry of movement and emotion. With roots dating back thousands of years, Bharathanatyam stands as a testament to the enduring power of expression through the human body.

THE SIGNIFICANCE OF NAMASKAR IN CLASSICAL DANCE

Before starting the dance and after the dance is over a dancer always does the namaskar. In Tamil it is known as Tatti Kumbidal which means stamp and bow down. It has deep meaning: the dancer prays to Mother Earth who is the supporter of all, who is worshipped by Devatas', who gives shelter. In devotion the dancer says, 'Oh Mother, you bear upon thyself the beat of my feet. Pray forgive me for the offence! In other words it is asking forgiveness for having stamped on Mother Earth. After salutations to Mother Earth the dancer goes on to seek the blessings of Gurus, learned Brahmins and the reverend Sabha.

What is the meaning of Saushtang

Saushtva + Anga - Proportionate body. There are set rules and regulations for a Bharatnatyam dancer while taking the basic pose. The posture in Bharatnatyam is called Aramandi or half-sitting. According to the rule the dancer will have to bend on both the feet keeping the knees pointing outwards, stiff body with a slight bend towards the front. If all these rules are fully followed the dancers *Srngaara haasya karuna*

NAVARASAM

Srngaara haasya karunaraudhra veera bhayaanakaah
beebhathsaadbhutha shaanthaashcha
rasaah poorvairudhaahrthaah

The Nine Sentiments The Erotic, the Comic, the Pathetic, the Furious, the Heroic, the Terrific, the Disgustful, the Wonderful and the Quietistic are the nine sentiments as told by the elders.

CHATHURTHABHINAYAS

Aangiko vaachikas thadhvath
Aahaaryas saathviko aparah chathurDhaa abhinayah
Thathra aangiko angair nidarshithah
Vaachaa virachithah kavyanaatakaadiShu vaachikah
Aahaaryo haarakeyoorave Shaadhibhir alankrithih
saathvikas saathvikair bhavaih bhaavajnena vibhaavithah

Abhinayas (Language of gestures)

The Abhinayas are four in number -aangika vaachika, aahaarya and saathvika. Here the 'aangika' is the one that is shown through limbs. That which is revealed through the words in poetry and drama is called 'vaachika' Aahaarya' is the one through dress, make up and ornaments.Saathvika' is the 'abhinaya' that is revealed through the expression of feelings.

Abhinaya in normal sense means facial expressions. On the stage where emotions are shown through face, eyes and sound it is abhinaya. Abhinaya literally means the representation or exposition of a certain theme from the Sanskrit word 'abhi' i.e. to or towards, with the root 'ni' i.e. to lead. Bharata explains Abhinaya as exhibiting the meaning of that which is depicted. Abhinaya has four aspectes namely 1) Angika abhinaya, 2) Vaachika abhinaya, 3) Aharya abhinaya, and 4) Satvika abhinaya

1) ANGIKA ABHINAYA: It is called angika as it is related to the body. The angas are the major limbs and upangas are the minor limbs. Angas are head, hands, chest, waist and feet. Upangas are eyes, eyebrows, nose, lips etc. and Pratyangas are shoulders, back, elbows, stomach portions, from knee to the heels etc. In angika abhinaya the facial expressions are not involved. The adavus and hasta mudras are examples of angika abhinaya.

2) VACHIKA ABHINAYA: Vachika abhinaya means"abhinaya through speech. Dramas use vachika abhinaya. In classical dance, Kuchipudi is one dance which uses vachika abhinaya to express abhinaya. In classical dance, though the dancer may not sing or"deliver speeches, the main singer gives expressions to the words of each song while the dancer interprets the meaning. This combination and understanding between dancer and musician is of extreme importance. Apart from beauty of the voice, clarity of word and bhava is necessary in dance and music in order that the audience be able to hear and comprehend each word of the song Then only it can be called Vachika abhinaya.

3) AHARYA ABHINAYA: The dress varies in each part of the country but it has to suit the time and place and the mood of the dance and drama. Dresses were even made suitable to sentiments and hence coloured accordingly. The make up and the costumes closest to Bharata's Natyashastra today are in Kathakali technique where characters are painted in different colours to suit their temperaments. In dance dramas settings are also used to bring out the Aharya abhinaya.

4) SATVIKA ABHINAYA Satvika abhinaya is very important for dance and drama. Satvika abhinaya means depicting or acting a state of mind which is caused by natural expressions or emotions. Satvika abhinaya is eight in number. They hold a middle place between the Sthayi and Vyabhichari bhavas. Satvika bhavas are: **i) Sthambha** (stupification). It is caused by joy, fear. disease, surprises, intoxication and anger. It is depicted in the form of immobility. **ii) Sveda** (sweat): It is caused by anger, fear, joy, weariness. It is depicted by fanning or wiping of perspiration. **iii) Romancha** (goose flesh): It is caused by touch, fear, cold etc. It is shown as though the hair are standing on their ends. **iv) Swara bheda** (change of voice): It is depicted by a choked voice caused due to fear, joy, anger or intoxication. **v) Vepatha** (trembling): It is shown by throbbing and shaking due to cold, fear, joy etc. **vi) Vaivarnya** (change of colour): It is depicted through weakness of limbs caused due to exertion or heat. **vii) Ashru** (tears): It is to be depicted by rubbing the eyes and shedding tears. **viii) Pralaya** (Loss of sense): It is to be depicted by falling on the ground due to weariness, sleep or injury. Navarasas like Shringara, veera, karuna, hasya, bhibhatsa, bhayanaka, adbhuta, raudra and shanta are also examples of Satvika abhinaya.

ANGAAAANI (LIMBS)

Angaaaani athra shiro hasthau

Vakshah paarshvau kateethatau

Padhau ithi shadukthaani

Greevaam api apare jaguh

Major limbs are six namely the head, the hands, the hip, the chest, the sides and the feet.Few opinion that neck to be included in this.

PRATHYANGAANI (ADDITIONAL LIMBS)

Prathyangaanyadha cha skandhau baahoo

Prshtam thathodharam

Ooroo janghe shadithyaahu apare

Manibandhakau

Jaanunee koorparaavethath

Trayamapyadhikam jaguh

Greevaasyathapi

The six limbs such as shoulders, arms , back , stomach, calves and shanks are known as prathyangaas.Wrist ,elbows,knees and neck are included by some writers.

UPAANGAANI (AUXILIARY LIMBS)

Upaanganthu skandha eva jagurbhudham

Drishthirbhroopuda thaarashcha kapolau nasika hanoo

Adharo dhashanaa jighua chubukam vadanam thathaa

Upaangaani dhvaadhashaiva

Shirasi angaanthreshu cha

Paashnigulphau thathaa

Angulyaah karayoh paadhayostale

Etani purvasastranusarenktani vai maya
Nrityammathropayogini kadhyathe lakshanai kramaath
Anganam calanaadeva prathyangopangayorapi
Chalanam prabhave tasmath sarvesham naathra lakshanam

The auxiliary limbs are shoulder only say pundits.The eyes, eyebrows, eyeballs, cheeks nose, jaw ,lowerlip , teeth, toungue, chin and face.These are twelve in number. There are others such as heels angles toes fingers etc of other parts. These things as explained in shastras are elaborated by me.These limbs are to be utilized in every performance.The movement of the minor limbs should be in accordance to the movement of major limbs .Hence all the movements are not elaborated in detail.

ASHTANAAYIKA AT A GLANCE

Thathra vaasakasajjaa vaa
virahothkhantithaapi vaa
svaadheenapathikaa vaapi
kalahaantharithaapi vaa
Khandithaa vipralabdhaa vaa
thathaa proShithabharthrkaa
Thatha abhisaarikaa chaiva
ithyashtau naayikaah smrthaah

HEROINES ARE OF EIGHT KINDS, AS FOLLOWS

Vaasakasajjika:- The dressed up heroine who awaits her lover.
Virahothkhanthitha :- the heroine in distress due to the non-arrival of her lover.

Svaadheenapathika:- confident of her lover.

Kalahaantharitha:- the quarrelsome heroine who later repents for the quarrel,

Khanditha:- the angered heroine whose husband is unfaithful.

Vipralabdha:- the disappointed heroine who has been deceived by her lover.

Proshithabhartrka:- the lovelorn heroine"whose husband is away.

Abhisaarika: - the heroine who goes to her"lover at any cost.

NAME FIVE JAATHIS AND SEVEN THALAAS OF CARNATIC MUSIC

Five jaathis

1.Thisra :- 3 mathra   :- Tha -ki-ta

2.Chathurasra:-4 mathra:- Tha -ka- dhi- mi

3.Khanda:-5 mathra:- Tha-ka- tha-ki-ta

4.Mishra:-7mathtra:-Tha- ki-ta-tha-ka-dhi-mi

5.Sankirna:-9 mathra:-Tha- ka-dhi-mi-tha-ka-tha-ki-ta

Seven thalas:-

1.Dhruva thala

2.Matya thala

3.Rupaka thala

4.Jhampa thala

5.Ata thala

6.Triputa thala

7.Eka thala.

The names of the five fingers

1.Angushta:-Thumb

2.Tharjini :-pointing finger

3.madhya or jeshtha:-the middle finger

4.Anamika:- the ring finger

5.Kanishta:-smallest finger.

SHORT NOTES

1) **BHAVA**:Bhava is the visual expression by which a dancer can convey the innerfeelings to the spectators without the use of speech or any mudras. Bhava is visible.The act of crying, conveying sadness are felt by the dancer.

2) **RASA**:Rasa is an obstract thing which cannot be seen or touched it can only be experienced both by the dancer and spectators.The rasa of the spectators is evoked by the bhava expressed by the dancer.Bhava and Rasa go together.The bhava grows from Rasa.

3) **MANDALA:** Mandala means position.The various positions of the leg and formation in dance are called mandals.There are 10 different kinds of mandalas.

4) **ADAVU**:The Anga,prathyanga,upanga movements with rhythm and by following the rules and regulations of paadhabedha is called an adavu.

5)**THANDAVA**:It is a majestic powerful vigirous masculine external dance with which depects the creation maintenance and dissolution of the universe , it is a virile dance mostly suitable for man.

6) LASYA: Lasya is a famine counterpart of the thandava.It is a graceful dance generally having Sringara as the dominant rasa.

7) RAGA: The combination of swaras which are melodious and are capable of pleasing the ears constitute a raga.It is a set of bnkites which pleases the ears.

8)THEERMANAM: A particular kind of adavu which is repeated in odd numbers or in multiples of 3 at the end of a jathi or a dance sequence.

9) SOLLUKATTU: Usinga a Thathkara with the combination of adavus and mridangam jathis is called sollukattu.

10) JATHI:A combination of 2 or more adavus with an intricate pattern of footwork and handmovements always ending with the theermanam.

11) CHARI: Walk or Gait for human beings (with music) in different meters with thaala.

12) JAATHI: The counting of laghu is 'jaathi'

13) GATHI: The gap between one beat and another rbeat in a thala is called 'Gathi'.

14) NADAI: How to use 'Gathi' in thala is 'Nadai'

ORIGIN OF NATYA (MYTHOLOGICAL)

Towards the end of trithvayug,there was a lot of miseryand suffering people had started disobeying the laws of nature people were selfish,greedy and power crazy.There was constant conflict between Devas and Asuras.So all the devas went to Lord Brahma went into deep meditation recollecting the four vedas , created the fifth veda called 'NATYAVEDA' in order to uplift the spirit of the people,so that they lead a dharmic life. He took words from Rigveda, music from Samaveda, bhava form Yejurveda and rasa(aesthetic feeling) from Atharvaveda. Brahma taught his Natyaveda to Bharathamuni in turn taught this to his hundred sons, who where endowed with Grahana (intelligence), Dharana (retension),Gnyana (knowledge) prayog (expression). Bharathamuni's sons could not able to learn the delicate style (kaishiki vruthi) of dance.On his request Brahma created 24 upsaras(Nymphs) and kaishiki vruthi was taught to these upsaras.

During the festival of 'Indhradhwaja', Bharathamuni staged a drama 'ASURAPARAJAI' (Defeat of the demons) asuras on seeing this performance where very offended(hurt) and started disturbing the drama.Brahma called the asuras to know why they where troubling the devas asuras told Brahma that they did not approved of only devas learning natya,Brahma was being partial to devas.Brahma smiled at them and explained that natya was ceated for everyone on earth and so anyonw could learn it whoever wished to do so.Thus there was peace now.

Bharathamuni then performed a drama called 'TRIPURA DAHANAM' in front of lord shiva.Shiva was filled with happy and immensely impressed by the drama.He requested his attendent Thandu to teach them (100 sons) his dance.As this dance was taught by Thandu,it came to be called as 'THANDAVA NRITHAM'. Lasya the other aspect of Shiva's dance was taught to Parvathi to the world.Usha he daughter of Banasura was a great devotee of Parvathi and so pleased with her devotion.Parvathi taught the lasya aspect to Usha . Usha inturn taught all her friends in Dwaraka,.This is how dance came to his mortal wolrd.

REPERTOIRE (Margam)

The fixed number of items decided by the old guru for a programme of Bharatanatym is called a Margam.In a Margam items are (1) Allaripu (2) Jathiswaram (3) Shabdham (4) Varnam (5) Padam (6) Thillana. Margam literally means the path or road. Since Bharatanatym was performed in temple by the Devadasis , Margam took them closer to the Almighty. This was a worship through which the Nartaki attained the devine ecstacy of body and soul.Through this path there is a union of Jeevatma and Paramatma. The dancer after learning a margam attains the basic knowledge of Nritta Nritya and Natya aspects of Bharatanatymn. A versatile dancer has knowledge of many such margams.As allaripu can be composed in all five Jathis ,jathiswaram can be composed in any Carnatic raga ,Shabhdam and Varnam can be composed according to any krithis by great poets and musicians. Thillanas are also in varied raaga patterns.Padam can be dance din any language slogams are based mainly on bhakthi dedicate to god and goddess and the end of a aBharatanatym performance there is aa Mangalam.The beginning of the program is always with an invocation to Lord Ganesha the elephant headed god and the destroyer of all obstacles.

ALLARIPU:It is the beginning ofa Bharathanatyam performance and it is the shortest dance. This is the beginning of basic movements of head, neck, and shoulders. Through this dance item one can know how much control the dancerhas on these Upangas. Allaripu literally means flowering ;as we offer flowers during the Pujas. The same way the dancer is offering her dance to the Lord of dance NATARAJA. The dancer with folded hands is invoking the Ashtadikhpalas and the Rangaadhidevatha. With Anjali hastha above her head she is invoking the gods,near the face she is invoking the Gurus andnear the chest she is invoking the learned Brahmins and sabha;the audience. This is an example of shudha NRITTA. Allaripu can be danced in five jathis. The simplest is Tishra jathi. In Allaripu ,Sholkattu is important.

JATHISWARAM: After the very simple Allaripu, the dancer goes on to exhibither command over Angashudha,Thalashudha and clarity of Mudras.

Jathiswaram is a combination of jathis or time measures, and swaram or Melodic notes. This is also an example of shudha Nritta .Abhinaya does not hold any place in Jathiswaram. Jathiswaram can be composed in any Carnatic Raga.Taking the swaram of the particular raga Bharathanatyam Adavus are set in beautiful Tala patterns. Some of the common Jathiswarams are Kalyani, Vasantha, Chakravaakam, Saveri etc…

SHABDAM: Shabdam is an introduction to Abhinaya. This is the third item in a Bharathanatyam Margam.Through this dance the dancer brings out the Nritya aspect of Bharathanatyam. Nrithya means the piece where there is aspecific theme or story in it.In Shabdam the dancer according to the words of the song shows specific mudras with facial expressions. Different moods or Navarasas are used in this dance like Shringara, Veera, Karuna, Adbhuta, Bhayanaka, Hasya, Bibhatsa, Raudra and Santha. Shabdam is dedicated to Gods,Goddesses, Kings, or any popular personality.Shabdam means the song of praise. In Sanskrit, it is known as Kirtigana.The popular raga used in Shabdam is Kamboji and Tala is Mishrachappu. It is mostely divided into four paragraphs. After each paragraph Sanchari bhava is used. It begins with sholkettu. The first paragraph is known as Pallavi,the second as Anupallavi,Third as Charanam and the fourth as Anucharanam. The rasa is mostly Sringara by ending is always Bhakthi. It ends always with Salamura or Namasthuhe.Most of the shabdam are Telugu or Tamil , but now other languages are also taking its place.

VARNAM: Varnam is the most important item in Bharathanatyam. It tests the skill of a dancer. Varnam literally means colour. It is a joyous combination of the three components namely Nritta,Nrithya and Natya. Varnam is dedicated to either Gods or Kings.In this importance is given to Sringara rasa. A versatile dancers favourite dance is varnam .With experience and practise Varnam gives brighter colours.Varnam is basically divided into two parts.First deals with Pallavi, Anupallavi, Chittaswaram and Sahithyam based on swarams.The second part deals with Charanam and three swarams and Sahithyam based on these swarams. The beginning of Varnam is with Mukkal thirumaanam and their abhinaya is shown based on the sahithyam. Whenever there is a thirumaanam or swaram there is Nritta,whenever there is a padam there is Nrithya.Theme of Varnams are usually Viraha, wherein Nayika is waiting for the beloved. Philosophically it is the longing of the Jeevatma to meet Paramaatma. In olden times Varnams were danced for one and hours to two hours but now it is reduced to 25-30 minutes.

PADAM: With padam intense abhinaya starts.It can be classified into Padams,kirthanams and Javali.When Sringara rasa is predominant,it is called padam. Some of the popular padams are of love songs of Radha and Krishna.When bhakthi is predominant it is called Kirtanams.In padams according to the meaning ,hastha mudras are performed with the appropriate rasas. Inolden times padams were danced in Tamil,Telugu and Kannada. In padams Nayika is presented as Virahotkhanditha, Khanditha, Abhisarika etc..

SHLOKAM: Shlokam are descriptive pieces of abhinaya.In this the use of Talam is not there.

THILLANA: Thillanais the last item in a Margam.It is a joyous ecstacy of scintillating rhythm,varied tala patterns and sculpturous poses. The Adavus are composed in vilambitha ,Maddhyama and dhruthalaya.In five jathis according to the melodic note of the ragas .Thillana is divided into five parts (1)Mai Adavu (2) Korvai, (3)Peria adavu, (4) Anthara, (5) Sahithyam.

MANGALAM: Mangalam is thanks giving to Gods and sabha for the success programme.It is composed by Saint poet Thyagaraja. In Mangalam there is no movement.Keeping hand on the hips or with folded hands the dancer stamps her feet and at the end of it there is Namashkar.

ORCHESTRA IN BHARATHANATYAM RECITAL

The orchestra which accompanies a bharathanatym recital ususally consists of the vocalist , Nattuvangam (cymbals), Mridnagam, Violin, Flute, Veena and in olden times the Clarionetand Mughaveena.

Earlier the Nattuvanar the teacher playing the cymbals and the drummer would move back and forth on the stage along with the dancer. But now the orchestra is placed on the right side or in the front (the orchestra platform).

NATTUVANGAM

The guru/teacher plays the cymbals (nattuvangam). The cymbal that is held on the one hand is bigger and made of iron while the one that is use dto strike is smaller and made of heavier bronze (panchaloka).Playing the cymbals is believed to guide the feet of the dancer.There are two aspects involved in playing the cymbals: Vallinam strong and Mellinam gentle.This is considered important while playing for both nritha and abhinaya.

MRIDANGAM

Mridangam plays a very important role in the orchestra .It speaks the sollu or the rhythamic syllables and enhances the beauty of nritha sequences.It gives that added effect to the performance, which is vital to the success of the recital.Special effects during abhinaya exposition are also achieved with the mridangam. A hollow cylindrical instrument (length approximately 24 -30 inches).The mridangam is made for the seasoned wood of the jackfruit tree. The rim of the two mouths are of buffalo skin held together by the string (vaaru) also of buffalo skin. The hollow on both sides is covered by cow-hide. On one side ,a black paste of rock powder and steamed rice is applied which when dried, produces the sound naadam. The musicians applies wheat flour (rava) on the other side to balance the base.

Veena :- The veena is a classical instrument that adds melodic richness to bharathanatyam . It is a plucked instrument with resonating strings and is played by a Veena artiste. The veena's soothing tones complement the dance and Vocal music.

Flute:-The flute, a woodwind instrument is usedto create melodious tunes in Bharathanatyam It's airy, ethereal sounds adds depthond imotion to the musical compositions. A skilled flutist plays the flute deering performances.

Violin:- The Violin is another essential instrument in Bharathanatyam, often accompan vocalists, and Providing melodic support.it is favored for its versatality and ability to mimic the nuances of vocal music. These musical instruments, along with Vocalists and Nuttuvanar, collectively create the musical backdrop for Bharathanatyam. Their harmonious interplay ensures that the dance form remains a mutlysensory experience, captivating both the eyes and ears of the audience.

MUSIC - AN INTEGRAL PART OF DANCE

Any discussion on dance will be incomplete without a study of music. Dance is but visual music and music is another form of expression like dance In India both music and dance have a strong spiritual background and both have been given a Divine origin . Music is one of the 4 upavedas(secondary vedas) and it is firmly believed that through musical meditation (Nadopasana) one can attain the supreme bliss. God is himself considered as the NadaBrahmam the very embodiment of sound 'Nada'.This chapter is primarily concerned with the aspect of indian music with respect to indian dance.the basis of all music is the Saptaswaras or the seven notes.Indian music is based on the principal of complete melody. Both the system of Indian music Carnatic and Hindustani, are based on extensive Raga and Thala systems.

Raga is the melodic aspect and paves the way for a creative expression of the singer laong systamatuic lines. Thala is the time measure which is a very importatnt aspect of Bharathanatyam. It is Thala which gives a sense of stability and form to both music and dance. GAMAKA, is the very essence of the melodic system is the 'graceful touch given to a note or a group of notes that emphasizes the melodic individuality of raga'.Music provides the life for dance. Both music and dance strive to depict a certain idea or story .Infact music has a responsible function for dance that merely assisting it.It strives to fill the gaps and pauses and creates the appropriate mood for dance. 'Sangitha' a term connecting music encompassed with vocal music,instrumental music and dance.

Geetham vaadhym cha nrityam cha
thrayam sangeethamuchyathe

It is essential for a dance choreographer to have a knowledge of music and its nuance.Proper ragas and thalas have to be chosen according to the mood to be portrayed.In a situation where pathos or devotion dominates,one cannot have music that excites or is war like which is contrary to the mood.

A music composer also needs to have the knowledge of dance and its intiricacies to comnpose music for dance.Vocal music plays a dominant role in indian dance especially in bharathanatayam while the percussion instruments provide the rhythamic assistance to the dance.Music shouldnot undermine the importance of dance.There are passages of silence that add to the dramatic effects of the situation this is also reffered to as rhythm in silence.

RENOWNED GURUS OF BHARATANATYAM

1) BALASARASWATI: Balasaraswati holds a supreme place in the field of dance. She was also a singer. She used to sing and dance Padams. Her 'Krishna ne begane padam dedicated to Lord Krishna was a legendary piece She was the last Devadasi. She sacrificed her life for the revival of Bharatanatyam. She had a great mastery over abhinaya. Both Indians and foreigners have a great reverence for this great dancer. She has toured all over the world for performances. Dancing had come to her through her mother Jayamala who was a great singer. She was born on 13th of May, 1918. She started learning dance at a very tender age. Her first Guru was Shri Kandapa who was a descendent of Chinniah Pillai. Along with dancing, her mother taught her Carnatic music. After seven years of rigorous training Balasaraswati did her Arangetram in

Kanchipuram Amnakshi temple. Her arangetram was well appreciated by the scholars, critics and common audience. At that time professional dancing was looked down upon and dancers did not enjoy a place in society. But Balasaraswati did not care about society She was adamant about popularising classical Bharatanatyam and she worked hard to bring a revolution in society She was the first dancer to bring Bharatanatyam out of the walls of the temple and present it to the public. This shows her knowledge of art, talent, courage, intelligence and determination. Throughout her lifetime she taught dance in the Madras Academy. For her meritorious service to art, she received the President's award and Padma Bhushan.

2) RUKMINI DEVI ARUNDALE: Rukmini Devi's arrival on the dance scene in the year 1935 opened a new chapter in the history of Bharatanatyam She was the daughter of a great Sanskrit scholar Shri Neelkanth Shastry and her mother was Seshammal who came from a learned family Rukmini Devi was the first Brahmin girl to take up dancing as a profession. She had her training under Pandanallur Meenakshi Sundaram Pillai, Mylapore Gauriamma and Muthukumar Pillai She started the world famous Kalakshetra in Madras and there her gurus themselves taught in the initial years. She gave her first public performance in March 1936. She also gave a recital at the Nataraj Temple at Chidambaram After her example, girls from Brahmin and other well to do families started taking up dance and Bharatanatyam was then considered as the rich cultural heritage of India. She was the first person to correlate the theory and practice of dance and music, thus making a significant revivalist movement. She designed the costumes artistically and temple jewellery was mostly used. She laid emphasis on the spiritual aspect of dancing. She practised dance dramas of high aesthetic. standard. Undoubtedly she was a great servant of art. She has succeeded in giving dance a place of pride in national life. She has been duly honoured with several awards and titles.

MEENAKSHI SUNDARAM PILLAI: Meenakshi Sundaram Pillai hails from Pandanallur Parampara, so his style of Bharatanatyam is known as Pandanallur style. He was given the title of Sangeeta Vidwan. His forefather was Sivananda Pillai who was one among the originator of Bharatanatyam. He comes from the family of Nattuvanars who had trained many Devadasis. Ponnaiah Pillai who was the gem of the Darbar of Sarfoji Maharaj and one who has given Bharatanatyam this new form is Meenaakshi Sundaram Pillai's maternal uncle. With this family background and gifted knowledge of theoretical and practical aspect of Bharatanatyam, he took the responsibility of the upliftment of Bharatanatyam His son Mutthaiah Pillai and his grandson Kittappa Pillai are keeping the family tradition alive Kittappa Pillai has established himself as one of the foremost Gurus of Bharatanatyam and he is carrying on the work of propagating Bharatanatyam in the cities of Bangalore and Madras. Meenakshi Sundaram Pillai died thirty years back. His son-in-law Chokalingam Pillai is also carrying on the work he has left. This great Guru will be remembered as the scholar of Pandanallur style of Bharatanatyam. He was generous in teaching and broad minded in sending his students to other Gurus for furthering their knowledge.

KUBERNATH TANJOREKAR: He is one of the great Grus of Tanjavore style. He hails from Tanjavore. He is well versed in music, dance and Mridangam. He is trained in Nattuvangam by great Guru Meenakshi Sundaram Pillai. He had his Carnatic music training from Shri Balakrishna Pillai and Hindustani music"from Faihaz Khan He has composed many traditional dances and his compositions are appreciated by class and mass equally. He was a professor of Bharatanatyam in Baroda music college. After retirement he is training many aspirants of dance who wants to take up dance as a profession and wants to gain expert knowledge. He speaks Tamil, Marathi, Hindi and Gujarati and composed Bharatanatyam Padams in different languages. His contribution to Gujarat is immense. His favourite students are Madhu Patel, Pratibha Pandit and Eelakshi Ben Thakore. He has travelled all over the world with dancer Ramgopal and Smt. Saroj Khakar. His Karmabhoomi is Baroda. Even at this age he is teaching Bharatanatyam and he worships it.

DEFINITION OF NRITTA, NRITYA, AND NATYA

Nritta :-Nritta is a form of pure movements in dance. Angas and Upangas are used. Rhythmic patterns are used to bring out beauty. It however does not convey any meaning. Nritta gives tempo to the dance. Examples of Nritta in Bharatanatyam are Adavus, Korvai, Tirumanam, Allaripu, Jatiswaram and Tillana. Most of the folk dances come in the Nritta category.

Nritya:- Nritya includes rasa (aesthetic flavour and bhava 1.e. emotion). In this, abhinaya, the art of expression is important. In Nritya, there will be a song. The dancer depicts the meaning of the particular song with the help of Hasta mudras and facial abhinaya. It will have a speicific theme. Navarasas are the examples of Nritya. In short Nritya is basically abhinaya. In Bharatanatyam Shabdam, Padam, Keertanam and Shlokam come in the category of Nritya. In Varnam one has both Nritta and Nritya. Wherever there is Tirumanam and Swaram, Nritta is used and wherever there is Sahityam, Nritya is used.

Natya:- The word natya is derived from Nata - i.e. acting. Natya means dramatic representation or drama with speech, music and dancing. It has a specific theme where each person performs his own role in the theme. There is a dialogue or song which the characters say or sing.Sometimes settings are also used in Natya. This indicates that in Natya one needs more than one person. The examples of Natya are Bhagavatamela natakam, Kuchipudi, Kuravanji etc. Natya is elaborate where there is the beginning, a climax and then an end to the story.

NATYASHASTRA

This is the most authentic and useful text which all classical dancers follow, all forms of classical dance have originated from this text.This valuable book is written by a sage Bharata.This book is also in the forms of shlokas and is written in Sanskrit. Natyashastra throws a light on all minute points: about how a stage should be erected ,where the artist should stand, the position of the vocalists and the precussionists and other details.The qualities of a prospective dancer has been given vividly like ,the dancer should not be very tall or very short, She should not be too stout or too thin , she should have big eyes, she should not be very fair or very dark. She should have a very sweet voice,so on and so forth. Even the accompaniments needed for dance is also mentioned like different types of melodious vadyas and different varieties of stringed vadyas. So we get details of dance music and drama from Natyashastra. It is said that Brahma has made four vedas and he took the most beautiful things from these vedas and created the fifth veda which is Natyaveda for the recreation of mind and body and gave it to Bharatamuni and he in turn put it in a systematic way and the text is known as Natyashastra.

Natyashastra have almost 1000 shlokas which has made Bharatamuni immortal.Bharatanatyam is named after this great sage writer Bharata. Bharatanatyam is based on the Bharata's natyshastra.So this dance form is called Bharatanatyam. Lord Shiva gave the knowledge of dance to Bharata and Parvati on other hand gave him the knowledge of Lasya and Bharata put this divine knowledge in systematic manner in his text Natyashastra and thus this divine knowledge came to us mortal .Accordingly to Natyashastra the first dance where performed by Devas and Asuras on the stage specially designed by Viswakarma. Natyashastra also tells us how dance schools should be and how a dance programme should begin. That is why we start our program with an invocation to Lord Ganapati and Rangadi devata, to the Gurus and accompanists. Navarasas are vividly described in addition to Hastamudras, talas, angika, abhinaya etc. Natyashastra deals with all aspects of dance and drama whereas Abhinaya Darpan deals only with dance. Natyashastra is nearly 4000 years old.

ABHINAYADARPAN : This text was written by Nandikeshwara in Sanskrit. This gives a vast knowledge of Angika abhinaya . It's a wonder that thousands of years ago a book with a systematic knowledge of writer . All classical dances of India are following the rules laid down by this text.

Even the minute details of Dance is described in this text like Chari. The different types of circular movements, Grivabedha i.e. neck movements, shirobedha i.e. Head movements, Drishtibedha i.e. eye movement and Hasthabedha i.e. Hand movements and its usages. Devata hasta hand movements are used for God Dashavathar hasta are the mudras for the ten incarnation of Vishnu. Kututmb hasta mudras relating to the relative like Father, Mother, Sister, Brother, Husband etc. Even the mudras for Brahmins, Kshatriyas, Vaishyas and Shudras are shown. Navagraha Hasta is also mentioned in this text. In addition to this the textalso tells us the qualities needed for a hero and heroine. That is the reason why all Indian classical dance forms are based on this text. Abhinaya Dharpan literarily means Abhinaya i.e acting and Dharpana means mirror,the mirror in which one can see the reflection of usage of Angas and Upanga.Not only Bharatanatym but also Manipuri, Kathakali, Oddissi and other forms of dance observe this as basic text. It is amazing that the though the text for all classical dances are same, each classical form differs in the technique and each has it's own characteristics and depth. So this text is a blessing for a student of classical dance and is a treasure presented to us by Nandikeshwara. Different people have different view about the time and author of this text. Some feels that according to Linga Purana , Nandikeshwara was the son of a blind woman who had prayed for a virtous son and the lord blessed her with a scholarly son. She named him Nandi and later he came to be known as Nandikeshwara, who had a vivid knowledge of dance, music, literature, and love for beauty. But some others say that Tandu may be Nandikeshwara.

BHARATHAARNAVA:-This is the most valuable for shuddha nrithya and angika abhinaya.It is written in Sanskrit in the form of slokhas or verse. Sree Nandikeshwara is considered as the foremost scholar in dance, music, stage craft and literature.Hastha mudras or hand gestures form the language of Indian dance.we get a detailed account of thehastha mudras from this book.

Both Abhinayadarpana and Bharathaarnava are ascribed to Nandikeshwara. Brahma went into deep meditation and out of all the four vedas drew a fifth veda the Natya veda.This veda was hundred over to Bharatha.Bharatha went to seek the help of Shiva for the steps. Shiva taught the steps to his disciple Thandu.Thandu is considered as Nandikeshwara. Bharatharnava is a beautiful piece of literature where Natya, Kavya, Gita, Nruthya. Navarasa and Abhinaya is depicted.The original book comprised of 4000 slokha but now only 800 slokhas are known as the book is not available. Shree vasudev shasthri has compiled this book . It is very useful for a student of Bharathanatyam.

Bharathanatyam gives stress to Rasotpathi. For example while doing sringara rasa the eyes should be in kantha drushthi with a mild saachidrushti with a smiling faceand neck in sundari. Thus Bharathaarnava have a very detailed account of the Rasashasthra.

SANGITA RATNAKARA

The author of Sangita Ratnakara is Sarangdeva. He was a Kashmiri. But his father had settled in South India. He was rendering his service to the King of Devagiri. From childhood Sarangdev took keen interest in Sanskrit. This was written in 13th centuary. It is very valuable for musicians and dancers alike. It is divided into 7 chapters.

1. Swaradyaya: Deals with its features, origin, variation and alankara.

2. Ragadyaya classifications: Deals with raga its variations and

3. Prakiranadya: Deals with the song and the singer's quality.

4. Prabandadyaya: Deals with the composition of the songs

5. Taladyaya: Deals with the time measure

6. Vadyadyaya: Deals with musical instruments when and where to be played the qualities necessary for a musician.

7. Nrityadyaya: Which Has 40 slokas narrating the birthof natva, description of angas and upangas. Rasa Drushti. Nritya karanas. Angahara, Sthanaka and Chari.

ADAVU

An 'adavu' is the basic unit of dance in Bharatanatyam. Each adavu has a posture (Sthaanaka), a movement of the legs and feet (chaari) a decorative hand gesture (Nrththa-hastha) and the correct position of the hand throughout its movement (Hastha kshetra). "An adavu is that where the feet stamp, the body, waist, hands and feet coordinate in graceful movement. Among them, the 'aramandi' or the half sit plie in ballet, is a very important stance in Bharatanatyam. The popular list of adavu groups in practice today are fourteen in number.

1. Thattu adavu -Thai yaa thai yee
2. Naattu adavu -Thai yum dhat tha thai yum thaa haa
3. Pakka adavu:-Thaa thai thai tha
4. Kuthitha mettu adavu:-Thai haa thai hii
5. Kutha adavu or Etta adavu:-That thai thaa haa
6. Sarukkal adavu or Jark adavu:-Thai yaa thai yii
7. Uthplutha adavu:-Thalaangu(jump)
8. Kartari adavu:- Dhit thai yum tha thaathai
9. Bhramari adavu:-That thai thaam Dhit thai thaam.
10. Shimir adavu:-Thai thai dhath tham
11. Mandi adavu:-Thanguda thatha Dhinna
12. Thattu Mettu adavu:-Pancha Nada
13. Theermana adavu:- Thai dhi dhi thai
14. Mei adavu:-used in the begining of Jathiswaram and Thillana.

KARANAS IN BARATHANATYAM AND USAGES

In Bharatanatyam, Karanas are dynamic and intricate movement sequences that combine several basic dance units such as steps, gestures, and poses. Karanas are an essential part of the repertoire and contribute to the richness and beauty of this classical Indian dance form. They are typically used in storytelling and choreography to convey various themes and emotions. Here's a more detailed explanation of Karanas and their usages:

1. Definition of Karanas: Karanas are a set of 108 key movement patterns or poses that are integral to Bharatanatyam and other Indian classical dance forms like Kuchipudi and Odissi. "Each Karana consists of a combination of distinct actions, including footwork (adi), hand gestures (mudras), body positions, and facial expressions."Karanas are characterized by their fluidity, grace, and precision. Dancers must execute them seamlessly to create a visually captivating and expressive performance.

2. Usages of Karanas in Bharatanatyam: Narrative Expression: Karanas are used to narrate stories from Hindu mythology, epics, and other traditional tales. Dancers employ Karanas to portray characters, events, and emotions from these narratives.

Aesthetic Appeal: Karanas contribute to the visual beauty and artistic quality of a Bharatanatyam performance. Their intricate and graceful movements captivate the audience's attention.

Rhythmic Expression: Karanas are often synchronized with the rhythm of the accompanying music (usually Carnatic music) and percussion instruments like the mridangam. They add rhythmic complexity and visual interest to the dance.

Spiritual and Symbolic Significance: Many Karanas have symbolic meanings associated with Hindu spirituality and mythology. Dancers may use these movements to convey deeper philosophical or spiritual concepts. Transitions: Karanas are employed to transition between different dance movements, postures, and sequences. They serve as bridges that connect various parts of a performance.

Choreography: Choreographers use Karanas to design intricate dance sequences and compositions. The selection and arrangement of Karanas are crucial in creating a cohesive and engaging performance. Training and Skill Development: Learning and mastering Karanas is an essential part of a Bharatanatyam dancer's training. They help develop strength, flexibility, balance, and body control.

3. Preservation and Revival: Karanas were originally documented in the ancient text "Natya Shastra" by Sage Bharata. Over time, this knowledge was lost, but efforts have been made to reconstruct and revive Karanas based on ancient sculptures, texts, and oral traditions. Scholars, dancers, and institutions have worked to research and reconstruct Karanas, ensuring their preservation and continuity in Bharatanatyam. In summary, Karanas are intricate movement patterns in Bharatanatyam that serve multiple purposes, including storytelling, aesthetic expression, and spiritual symbolism. They are an integral part of the dancer's training and contribute significantly to the art form's depth and beauty.

108 KARANAS

1.Talapuspaputam 2.Varthitam 3.Valithorukam 4.Apavidham 5.Samanakham 6.Leenam 7.Swastikarechitham 8.Mandala swasthikam 9.Nikuttakam 10.Ardhanikuttakam 11.Kadichinnam 12. Ardharechitham 13. Vakshaswasthikam 14. Unmatham 15. Swasthikam 16. Prushtaswasthikam 17. Dikswasthikam 18. Alaatakam 19. Kadeesamam 20. Akshiptarechitham 21. Vikshipthakshiptham 22. Ardhaswasthikam 23. Anchitham 24. Bhujangatrasithkam 25. Urdhvajanu 26. Nikunchitham 27. Mathalli 28. Ardhamathalli 29. Rechithanikuttakam 30. Padapavidham 31. Valitham 32. Ghurnitham 33. Lalitham 34. Dandapaksham 35. Bhujangathrastharechitham 36. Nupuram 37.Vaishakharechitham 38.Bhramarakam 39. Chathuram 40. Bhujanganchitham 41. Dandarechitham 42.Vrischikakuttitham 43. Kadibhrantham 44.Lathavrischikam 45. Chinnam 46. Vrischikarechitham 47. Vrischikam 48.Vyamsitham 49.Parsvanikutitham 50. Lalatathilakam 51.Krantam 52. Kunchitam 53. Chakramandalam 54. Uromandalam 55. Akshiptham 56. Talavilasitham 57. Argalam 58. Vikshiptham 59. Avartham 60. Dolapadam 61. Vivrutham 62. Vinivritham 63. Parswakrantham 64. Nisumbhitham 65. Vidyutbhrantham 66. Athikrantham 67. Vivartithitam 68. Gajakreditakam 69.Talasamsphotitham 70.Garudapluthakam 71.Gandasuchi 72. Parivrutham 73.Parsvajanu 74.Grudravaleenakam 75.Sannatham 76. Suchi 77.Ardhasuchi 78. Suchividham 79. Apakrantham 80. Mayuralalitham 81.Sarpitham 82. Dandapadam 83.Harinaplutham 84.Premkholitham 85. Nitambham 86. Skhalitham 87. Karihastham 88. Prasarpitham

89. Simhavikreeditham 90. Simhakarshitham 91. Udrutham 92. Upasruthakam 93. Talasamghatitham 94. Janitham 95. Avahithakam 96. Nivesam 97. Edakakreeditham 98. Urudruthvam 99. Madaskalitham 100. Vishnukrantham 101. Sambhrantham 102. Vishkhambham 103. Udghattitham 104.Vrushabhakreeditham 105. Lolitham 106.Nagapasarpitham 107. Sakadasyam 108. Gangavatharanam

1.Talapuspaputam

2.Varthitam

3.Valithorukam

4. Apavidham

5.Samanakham

6.Leenam

7.Swastikarechitham

8.Mandalaswasthikam

9.Nikuttakam

10.Ardhanikuttakam

11.Kadichinnam

12. Ardharechitham

13. Vakshaswasthikam

14. Unmatham

15. Swasthikam

16. Prushtaswasthikam

17. Dikswasthikam

18. Alaatakam

19. Kadeesamam

20. Akshiptarechitham

21. Vikshipthakshiptham

22. Ardhaswasthikam

23. Anchitham

24. Bhujangatrasithkam

25. Urdhvajanu

26. Nikunchitham

27. Mathalli

28. Ardhamathalli

29. Rechithanikuttakam

30. Padapavidham

31. Valitam

32. Gurnitam

33. Lalitam

34. Dandapaksham

35. Bhujangathrastharechitham

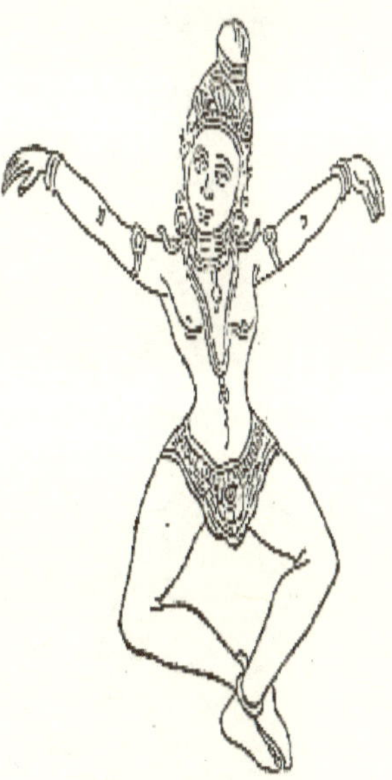

36. Nupuram

37.Vaishakharechitham

38. Bhramarakam

39. Chathuram

40.Bhujanganchitham

41. Dandarechitham

42. Vrischikakuttitham

43. Kadibhrantham

44.Lathavrischikam

45. Chinnam

46. Vrischikarechitham

47. Vrischikam

48. Vyamsitham

49. Parsvanikutitham

50. Lalatathilakam

51.Krantam

52. Kunchitam

53. Chakramandalam

54. Uromandalam

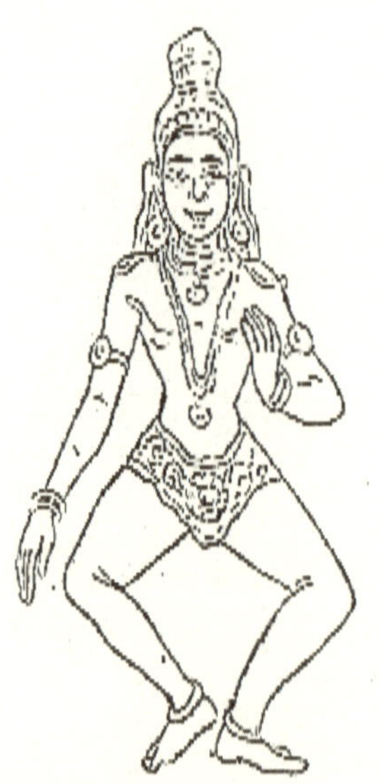

55. Akshiptham

56. Talavilasitham

57. Argalam

58. Vikshiptham

59. Avartham

60. Dolapadam

61. Vivrutham

62. Vinivritham

63. Parswakrantham

64. Nisumbhitham

65. Vidyutbhrantham

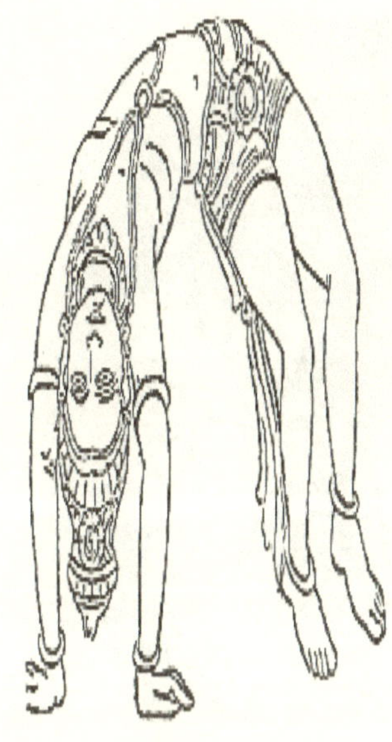

66. Athikrantham

67. Vivartithitam

68. Gajakreditakam

69.Talasamsphotitham

70.Garudapluthakam

71.Gandasuchi

72. Parivrutham

73.Parsvajanu

74.Grudravaleenakam

75.Sannatham

76. Suchi

77.Ardhasuchi

78. Suchividham

79. Apakrantham

80. Mayuralalitham

81.Sarpitham

82. Dandapadam

83.Harinaplutham

84.Premkholitham

85. Nitambham

86. Skhalitham

87. Karihastham

88. Prasarpitham

89. Simhavikreeditham

90. Simhakarshitham

91. Udrutham

92. Upasruthakam

93. Talasamghatitham

94. Janitham

95. Avahithakam

96. Nivesam

97. Edakakreeditham

98. Urudruthvam

99. Madaskalitham

100. Vishnukrantham

101. Sambhrantham

102. Vishkhambham

103. Udghattitham

104. vrusnabhakreedithnam

105. Lolitham

106. Nagapasarpitham

107. Sakadasyam

108. Gangavatharanam

BIBLIOGRAPHY

1. Dance gestures (Mirror of expressions). R. Ramachandra sekhar, Giri trading agency private limited 2007.

2. Abhinayadarpana. Trans Manomohan Ghosh. Calcutta: Manisha Granthalaya, 1975.

3. Padma Subrahmanyam. Natyasastra and National Unity Thrippunithura: Sri Ramavarma Govt. Sanskrit College, 1997.

4. Indian Theatre and Dance Traditions. Shovana Narayan, Delhi: Harman Publishing House, 2004.

5. Invitation to Indian Dancess. Susheela Misra, Eds New Delhi: Arnold Heinemann, 1987, Liverpool: Lucas, 1989.

6. Bharatanatyam in Tamilnadu R.Kalrani. Madurai JJ Publications, 2004.

7. Nandikeshwara. Abhinayadarpana. Trans. C Rajendran, Delhi: New Bharatiya Book Corporation, 2007.

8. Brahmanic Temple Institutions and their influence on Kerala Society. Raghava Varier, M.R., 1977, Term Paper submitted at Jawaharlal Nehru University.

9. Understanding Harappa Civilization in the Greater Indus Vallley, Ratnagar, Shereen, 2002, Delhi, Tulika.

10. Reform and Revival: The Devadasi and Her Dance. Srinivasn,Amrit 1985, Economic and Political Weekly 20 (44), pp.1869-76.

11. A Social History of Music in south India. Subrahmaniam, Lakshmi, 2006, From Tanjore Court tothe Madras Music Academy: Delhi, Oxford University Press.

12. Natyasastra and National Unity. Subrahmanyam, Padma, 1997, Tripunithura, Sree Ramavarma Govt. Sanskrit College.

13. Women Writing in India 600 BC to. Present. Tharu, Susi & K. Lalitha (eds.), 1998, Delhi, Oxford University Press.

14. Indian Classical Dance. Vatsyayan, Kapila, 1992, Delhi, Publication Division, Ministry of Information and Broadcasting, Govt. of. India.

15. Vaidhyanadha Aiyer, G.Tr. Pathittuppathu, Thrissur: Kerala Sahithya Academy,1997.

16. Wallace Dace, 1963,.The Concept of "Rasa" in Sanskrit Dramatic Theory. Educational Theatre Journal. 15 (3): 249. doi:10.2307/3204783 JSTOR 3204783 cc.

17. laghu bharatham, sudharani raghupathi, Govt. Of India, Ministry of HRD,1995 vol. I, II, III.

18.The classical dance poses of India:-Gopinath &S V Raman rao.

19.The Nattuvanar's Art:-Emily. N. Mayne